Object-Oriented Programming in Java

Lucien Sina

May 5, 2026

Contents

Preface

Welcome! This book was written with a clear goal in mind: to guide you through the foundational concepts of programming and steadily build up to the principles of object-oriented design, a paradigm essential for modern software development.

Programming is not just about writing code; it is about problem-solving, creating efficient solutions, and learning how to think logically and systematically. This book starts with the very basics—introducing what programming is, how algorithms are formed, and how Java, a versatile and widely-used language, can be your tool for implementing solutions.

As you progress through the chapters, you will explore essential programming constructs, such as loops, data types, and methods. Then, the book delves into the principles of object-oriented design, covering concepts like encapsulation, inheritance, polymorphism, and classification. Along the way, exercises, examples, and solutions will help reinforce your understanding and encourage you to apply what you've learned.

This book is designed for beginners, but it does not stop there. For those ready to take the next step, it offers a smooth transition into more advanced topics. Furthermore, I have included a glimpse into future books, such as one dedicated to advanced programming skills, another to algorithms and data structures, and a deeper exploration of theoretical topics like computability and complexity. These books are intended to complement this one, helping you grow as a programmer and problem-solver.

I hope this book serves as a helpful companion on your journey into programming. If you have any feedback, questions, or suggestions, please do not hesitate to reach out.

Happy coding!

Chapter 1

Problems, Algorithms, and Programs

1.1 Introduction

Every program begins with a problem. In programming, a problem is a task or question that requires a solution, and a program is the tool that provides this solution through a series of logical steps. The goal of this chapter is to introduce you to foundational concepts, problems, algorithms, and programs and provide an overview of programming languages and paradigms that influence how solutions are crafted and implemented.

1.2 What Is a Problem?

In programming, a problem is any task that we need to solve or any question that requires an answer. For example: How do I sort a list of numbers in order? or: How can I build software that helps manage inventory in a store?

A programming problem typically has:

Inputs: Data or information provided for the solution (e.g., a list of numbers). **Outputs**: The desired result (e.g., the list sorted in ascending order). **Constraints**: Rules or limits within which the solution must operate (e.g., the list should not exceed a certain length, or the sorting process should be efficient).

Exercise 1.1: Identify a real-world problem you encounter, like finding the shortest route to work. Identify:

The inputs The desired outputs Any constraints Solution to Exercise 1.1: Example: Planning the shortest route to work.

Inputs: Starting location, destination, traffic data. Outputs: The shortest route. Constraints: Minimize travel time, avoid tolls or closed roads.

1.3 Steps to Transform a Real-World Problem into a Program

The journey from a real-world problem to a working program involves a series of transformations:

Real-World Problem: Identifying the task we need to solve. **Abstraction**: Simplifying the real-world problem by focusing on relevant details while ignoring unnecessary ones. **Problem Description**: Describing the problem in general terms. **Precising and Formalization**: Refining the description to specify key details and requirements. **Problem Specification**: Clearly defining the inputs, outputs, and constraints. **Declaring the possible Solution Space**: Exploring potential ways to solve the problem. **Algorithm**: Creating a step-by-step plan for the solution. **Programming in a Higher-Order Language**: Translating the algorithm into a programming language. **Translation into Machine Code**: Converting the code into instructions that a computers hardware can execute. **Input**: Providing the data to the program. **Output/Result**: The program processes the input to produce the desired result.

Exercise 1.2: Think of a simple task, like baking a cake. Outline each step in transforming the task into a series of instructions a person could follow, similar to the steps above.

Solution to Exercise 1.2: Example: Baking a cake.

Real-world problem: Making a cake. Abstraction: Focus on necessary ingredients and steps only. Problem description: How to bake a cake? Precising: Specify cake type, ingredients, and baking method. Specification: Exact recipe with ingredients and steps. Solution: Identify all necessary steps (mixing, baking). Algorithm: Step-by-step instructions. Higher-order language: Recipe card or cooking instructions. Machine code: Actions performed by the baker. Input: Ingredients. Output: A freshly baked cake.

1.4 What Is an Algorithm?

An algorithm is a clear, step-by-step set of instructions designed to solve a problem. Think of an algorithm as a recipe: it is a sequence of steps you follow to achieve a specific result.

For example, if your problem is sorting a list of numbers, an algorithm provides the steps to arrange the numbers in order. Algorithms need to be:

Clear: Each step should be unambiguous and easy to understand. **Precise**: Every detail is defined with no ambiguity. **Efficient**: Ideally, the steps should lead to a solution in the most effective way possible.

Exercise 1.3: Write an algorithm for brushing your teeth. Each step should be clear and precise.

Solution to Exercise 1.3:

Pick up the toothbrush. Apply toothpaste to the brush. Place the toothbrush in your mouth. Move the brush over all teeth for two minutes. Rinse your mouth and the toothbrush.

1.5 What Is a Program?

A program is the implementation of an algorithm in a way that a computer can execute. Programs are written in programming languages, which let us translate algorithms into instructions a computer can understand. For instance, a program that sorts numbers would follow the steps of a sorting algorithm, expressed in a language that the computer can execute.

Programs consist of:

Code: Instructions written in a programming language. **Data**: Information processed by the program. **Logic**: Decision-making that determines the programs actions.

1.6 Programming Languages and Paradigms

Programming languages are tools we use to write programs, each with its own syntax (rules for writing instructions) and features. For instance:

Python: Known for its simplicity, making it ideal for beginners. **Java** (which we will use in this book): Known for its reliability and ability to run on multiple platforms.

Programming Paradigms A programming paradigm is a way of organizing and thinking about code. Different paradigms suit different types of problems, and understanding these paradigms helps us choose the best approach for a given task. Let us look at a few common paradigms:

-Imperative Programming: Writing sequences of instructions that tell the computer how to achieve a result. Examples include: **-Procedural Programming**:

Focusing on functions that perform operations in a sequence (e.g., steps to solve a math problem).

Object-Oriented Programming (OOP): Organizing code into objects that represent real-world things, like creating a library system with book and borrower objects. **Declarative Programming**: Focusing on **what** the result should be, leaving the **how** to the programming language or environment. Examples include:

Functional Programming: Defining operations as a series of functions, often without changing state or data. Common in mathematical applications, it emphasizes clear relationships between inputs and outputs. **Logic Programming**: Using logic and rules to specify desired outcomes. An example is Prolog, where relationships and facts are used to infer new information. **Aspect-Oriented Programming (AOP)**: Separating cross-cutting concerns (e.g., logging or error handling) to make code more modular and easier to maintain. AOP helps by isolating functionality that affects multiple areas of a program.

Exercise 1.4: Identify three different problems and think about which programming paradigm might best suit each. Justify your choices.

Solution to Exercise 1.4:

Sorting a list of numbers: Procedural, as it involves a straightforward sequence of steps. Inventory management system: Object-Oriented, since items and inventory operations can be represented as objects. Expert system for medical diagnosis: Logic Programming, as it can use rules and facts to infer possible diagnoses.

1.7 Summary

In this chapter, we defined the foundational elements of programming: problems, algorithms, and programs. We explored how a real-world problem is transformed into a programmed solution through a series of steps. We also introduced programming languages and paradigms, providing context for how programming approaches vary and why they are suited to different tasks. Now, with these core concepts in mind, you are ready to dive deeper into programming and start creating solutions!

Chapter 2

Setting Up Your Java Development Environment

2.1 Introduction

Before diving into Java programming, it's essential to set up a development environment to write, compile, and run Java code efficiently. In this chapter, we'll guide you through installing the Java Development Kit (JDK) and setting up an Integrated Development Environment (IDE). We'll cover two popular options, Eclipse and Android Studio, so you can choose the one that best suits your needs. By the end of this chapter, you'll have a complete environment ready for programming.

2.2 Installing the Java Development Kit (JDK)

The JDK is necessary for compiling and running Java programs, and it provides the core libraries needed to work with Java.

Step-by-Step Guide to Installing the JDK: Download the JDK:

Visit the official Oracle JDK download page or install OpenJDK from the OpenJDK website. Choose the latest JDK version compatible with your operating system (Windows, macOS, or Linux). Install the JDK:

Follow the installation instructions on the download page. Most installers offer a default path, which you can keep, or you can choose a custom path. Set Environment Variables (Windows only):

Open System Properties > Advanced System Settings > Environment Variables. Under "System Variables," find Path, select it, and click "Edit." Add a new path to your JDK's bin directory, for example

```
C:\Program Files\Java\jdk-xx\bin
```

Verify the Installation:

Open a terminal or command prompt and type java -version. If the JDK is installed correctly, you'll see the JDK version displayed. Exercise 2.1: Open your terminal or command prompt and run java -version and javac -version. Confirm that both commands recognize the Java installation. If you see version information, your JDK is installed correctly.

Solution to Exercise 2.1: If your installation was successful, you should see output similar to: java version "17.0.1" 2021-10-19 LTS Java(TM) SE Runtime Environment (build 17.0.1+12-39) Java HotSpot(TM) 64-Bit Server VM (build 17.0.1+12-39, mixed mode, sharing)

2.3 Choosing an IDE: Eclipse vs. Android Studio

An Integrated Development Environment (IDE) is essential for programming, as it provides tools to edit, compile, and debug code efficiently. Let's briefly compare Eclipse and Android Studio to help you choose the one that best meets your needs.

Eclipse:

Pros: Highly customizable, lightweight, popular for a wide range of Java applications. Cons: May require plugins for certain functionalities, less optimized for Android development. Best for: General Java development and larger applications.

Android Studio:

Pros: Excellent for Android development, includes Android-specific libraries and tools. Cons: Requires more system resources, best suited for Android-focused projects. Best for: Beginners interested in mobile app development with Java. Choose the IDE that fits your goals. If you're new to programming, you might find Eclipse's simpler interface easier to start with. If mobile app development interests you, Android Studio will provide a solid foundation.

2.4 Setting Up Eclipse

Step-by-Step Guide to Installing and Setting Up Eclipse Download Eclipse:

Go to the Eclipse download page. Select "Eclipse IDE for Java Developers" and download the installer for your operating system. Install Eclipse:

Run the downloaded installer and select the default installation options. Once installed, launch Eclipse. Create a New Java Project:

Open Eclipse and select File > New > Java Project. Name the project (e.g., "HelloWorld") and click "Finish." Write Your First Program:

Right-click on the src folder in the Project Explorer. Select New > Class, name it HelloWorld, and check "public static void main(String[] args)" to include the main method. Inside the main method, type:

```
public class HelloWorld {
    public static void main(String[] args) {
        System.out.println("Hello, World!");
    }
}
```

Save the file and run it by right-clicking and selecting Run As > Java Application. Exercise 2.2: Write and run your first "Hello, World!" program in Eclipse, following the steps above. Confirm that the output is displayed in the console.

2.5 Setting Up Android Studio

Step-by-Step Guide to Installing and Setting Up Android Studio Download Android Studio:

Visit the Android Studio download page and download the installer for your operating system. Install Android Studio:

Run the installer and follow the prompts to complete the installation. Android Studio will also download the necessary SDKs and tools for Android development. Create a New Project:

Open Android Studio and select New Project. Choose a project template, like "No Activity" for a simple Java program or "Empty Activity" if you're interested in Android apps. Name your project (e.g., "HelloWorld") and choose "Java" as the language. Write Your First Program:

In the project's main Java file, create a HelloWorld class (or edit the main activity for Android projects). In the main method, type:

```java
public class HelloWorld {
    public static void main(String[] args) {
        System.out.println("Hello, World!");
    }
}
```

If it's an Android app, you'll instead set up a TextView in the XML layout to display "Hello, World!" on the screen. Run Your Program:

For non-Android Java projects, run the program by right-clicking the main Java file and selecting Run. For Android apps, select Run > Run 'app' to test the app on an emulator or connected device. Exercise 2.3: Create and run your "Hello, World!" program in Android Studio. If working with an Android app, display the message on the screen using a TextView widget.

2.6 Troubleshooting Common Setup Issues

Setting up an IDE can sometimes lead to unexpected issues. Here are some common issues and solutions:

JDK Not Recognized: Ensure the JDK is installed correctly and environment variables are set (Windows users). IDE Crashes or Fails to Open: Check if your system meets the IDE's minimum requirements. Program Not Running: Double-check that the main method is correctly written as public static void main(String[] args). Ensure you're running the correct file. Tip: If problems persist, consult the official documentation or online forums for troubleshooting advice. Both Eclipse and Android Studio have large communities, so most issues have solutions posted online.

2.7 Summary

In this chapter, we've set up the essential tools needed for Java programming. Whether you chose Eclipse or Android Studio, you now have an environment where you can write, run, and troubleshoot Java code. This setup is the foundation for your journey into programming.

In the next chapter, we'll explore Java's program structure, learning about syntax diagrams, program headings, and other foundational aspects of Java code. Congratulations on getting set up and writing your first program!

Chapter 3

Understanding Java Program Structure

3.1 Introduction to Program Structure

A Java program has a specific structure that allows it to be compiled and executed. Understanding this structure will help you read, write, and debug code effectively. In this chapter, we'll break down the parts of a Java program, explore how to represent program syntax visually, and introduce key concepts like program headings, blocks, declaration parts, and statement parts.

3.2 Syntax Diagrams: Visualizing Java Syntax

Syntax diagrams (also called railroad diagrams) are a useful way to visualize the structure of programming languages. They illustrate the rules for combining elements in Java and help clarify how different components of code fit together.

Key Concepts: **Terminals**: Fixed elements in the language, like keywords (**class**, **public**, **static**) and symbols (, , ;), that must appear exactly as written. **Non-Terminals**: Variable elements representing placeholders or patterns that need to be filled with specific values, like identifiers (e.g., variable names) or expressions. Example: A syntax diagram for a Java class definition could show that a class starts with the keyword **class**, followed by an identifier (the class name), and then the code block ... .

3.3 Basic Structure of a Java Program

The structure of a Java program generally consists of the following key parts:

1. Program Heading (Class Definition):

Every Java program starts with a class definition. The program heading includes keywords like **public** and **class**, followed by the class name, and is the top-level structure. **Example:**

```
public class HelloWorld {
    // code block
}
```

Syntax Diagram for Class Definition

public (optional) -> class -> ClassName -> -> Code Block ->

Explanation:

public (optional): The access modifier, which is optional here. class: The keyword to define a class. ClassName: Placeholder for the name of the class (a non-terminal). : Curly braces enclose the Code Block, which contains the main body of the class.

2.Main Method (Program Entry Point):

The main method, public static void main(String[] args), is the entry point for Java programs. This method defines what the program will execute when run. **Example:**

```
public static void main(String[] args) {
    // statements
}
```

3.Code Block:

A code block is a section of code enclosed in , grouping statements or declarations. Blocks define the scope of code sections, meaning variables and statements within a block are only accessible within that block. **Example:**

```
public class HelloWorld {
```

```
    public static void main(String[] args) {
        System.out.println("Hello, World!");
    }
}
```

3.4 Declaration Part

The declaration part is where you define variables, constants, and other elements necessary for the program. Declarations typically appear at the start of a method or class, allowing you to organize information about the data before using it in statements.

Variables: Variables store data, which can change throughout the program's execution. Constants: Constants hold values that don't change. **Example:**

```
int age = 25; // variable declaration
final double PI = 3.14159; // constant
declaration
```

Syntax Diagram for Declaration:

A variable declaration might look like: [type] [variable name] [initial value (optional)]; Explanation:

Type: The data type (e.g., int, String). VariableName: Name of the variable being declared. = (optional): The assignment operator, used if there's an initial value. InitialValue (optional): An initial value for the variable. ;: End of the declaration.

3.5 Statement Part

The statement part includes executable statements that make the program do something, such as calculations, printing to the console, and making decisions.

Types of Statements: Assignment Statements: Assign a value to a variable.

```
int number = 5;
number = number + 1;
```

Syntax Diagram for Assignment Statement VariableName -> = -> Expression -> ;

Explanation:

VariableName: The variable to which a value is being assigned. =: Assignment operator. Expression: Value or calculation assigned to the variable. ;: End of the statement.

Control Statements: Include conditionals (if, else) and loops (for, while) to control the flow of the program.

```
if (number > 0) {
    System.out.println("Positive number");
}
```

Syntax Diagram for If...Else Statement if -> (Condition) -> StatementBlock -> (else -> StatementBlock (optional))

Explanation:

if: Keyword to start the conditional statement. (Condition): Boolean condition to evaluate. StatementBlock

: Block of code to execute if the condition is true. else (optional): Optional keyword to specify alternative code to execute if the condition is false. StatementBlock : Block of code to execute if the else condition is met.

Syntax Diagram for While Statement while -> (Condition) -> StatementBlock

Explanation:

while: Keyword for the loop. (Condition): Boolean expression controlling loop execution. StatementBlock : Block of code to repeat while the condition is true.

Syntax Diagram for For Loop he for loop in Java has three main parts within its parentheses:

Initialization (typically used to initialize a counter variable), Condition (the loop runs as long as this condition is true), Update (executed after each iteration).

for -> (Initialization ; Condition ; Update) -> StatementBlock

Explanation:

for: Keyword to start the loop. (Initialization ; Condition ; Update): Parts within parentheses, separated by semicolons: Initialization: Usually a variable declaration or counter initialization (e.g., int i = 0). Condition: Boolean expression that must be true for the loop to continue. Update: Expression that updates the loop variable (e.g., i++). StatementBlock : Block of code to execute each time the loop iterates.

Example:

```
for (int i = 0; i < 5; i++) {
    System.out.println(i);
```

```
}
```

Method Calls: Call a method to perform a specific action.

```
System.out.println("Hello, World!");
```

Syntax Diagram for Method Call Statement:

ObjectOrMethodName -> (Arguments (optional)) -> ;

Explanation:

ObjectOrMethodName: Name of the method (or object with a method). ( ): Parentheses around any arguments passed to the method. Arguments (optional): Values to pass to the method. ;: End of the statement.

3.6 Putting It All Together: Example Program Structure

Here's an example Java program that demonstrates all these components together. We'll use comments to label each part.

```
// Program heading (class definition)
public class Example {

    // Declaration part
    // constant declaration
    static final double PI = 3.14159;
    // main method (entry point):
```

```
    public static void main(String[] args) {

        // Declaration part
        int radius = 5; // variable declaration

        // Statement part
        // assignment statement:
        double area = PI * radius * radius;
        // method call (output statement):
        System.out.println("Area: " + area);

        // Control structure (if statement)
        if (area > 10) {
            System.out.println("Large area");
        } else {
            System.out.println("Small area");
        }
    }
}
```

3.7 Exercise: Creating a Program Structure

In this exercise, you'll create a simple Java program with a class definition, a main method, a declaration part with variables and constants, and a statement part that includes output and a control structure.

Exercise Steps:

Define a class named BasicProgram. Inside the class, define the main method. In the main method, declare a variable number and assign it a value. Use an if statement to check if number is greater than 0. If so, print "Positive number"; otherwise, print "Non-positive number".

Solution:

```java
public class BasicProgram {
    public static void main(String[] args) {
        int number = 10; // Declaration part

        // Statement part
        if (number > 0) {
            System.out.println("Positive number");
        } else {
            System.out.println("Non-positive number");
        }
    }
}
```

3.8 Summary

In this chapter, we explored the structure of Java programs and used syntax diagrams to visualize different parts. We learned about program headings, blocks, declaration parts, and statement parts, building a foundation for understanding Java syntax and program flow.

This structure will guide us as we dive deeper into Java programming concepts in the following chapters.

Chapter 4

Identifiers and Numbers

In programming, identifiers and numbers form the building blocks for naming and handling data. This chapter introduces these concepts, covering the rules for identifiers and the different types of numbers in Java.

4.1 Identifiers

Identifiers are names given to elements in a program, such as variables, methods, classes, and other structures. These names allow programmers to reference specific parts of the code with meaningful, readable labels.

Rules for Naming Identifiers: In Java, identifiers must follow specific rules:

Allowed Characters: Identifiers can only contain

letters (A-Z and a-z), digits (0-9), underscores ("_"), and dollar signs ("$"). Starting Character: Identifiers cannot begin with a digit. They must start with a letter, underscore, or dollar sign. No Reserved Words: Keywords or reserved words (like int, class, for, if, etc.) cannot be used as identifiers. Case Sensitivity: Java is case-sensitive, so Variable, variable, and VARIABLE would each be recognized as different identifiers. Examples of Valid Identifiers:

```
myVariable,
sum_of_values,
MAX_VALUE,
\$totalCount
```

Examples of Invalid Identifiers:

```
3rdPlace (starts with a digit),
int (reserved keyword),
price# (contains an illegal character, #)
```

Using descriptive and meaningful identifiers is encouraged to make code more readable. Instead of vague names like x or y, identifiers like totalScore or customerAge make the purpose of the variable clear.

4.2 Numbers

In Java, numbers are classified by their data types. Each type supports a certain range of values and determines how much memory is allocated for that value.

Integer Numbers: Integer numbers represent whole numbers, both positive and negative. Java has four integer types:

byte: A small integer, ranging from -128 to 127. It's commonly used to save memory in large arrays. short: A slightly larger integer than byte, ranging from -32,768 to 32,767. int: The most commonly used integer type, ranging from -2,147,483,648 to 2,147,483,647. long: A large integer type, ranging from -9,223,372,036,854,775,808 to 9,223,372,036,854,775,807. Suffix L or l is required for long literals, as in 123456789L. Floating-Point Numbers Floating-point numbers represent decimal values and support fractional parts. Java has two types of floating-point numbers:

float: A single-precision 32-bit number with a range of approximately 1.4E-45 to 3.4E+38. Suffix F or f is required for float literals, as in 3.14F. double: A double-precision 64-bit number with a range of approximately 4.9E-324 to 1.8E+308. This is the default type for decimal values. Numeric Literals Numeric literals are constant values written directly in the code. They represent integer or floating-point values.

Integer Literals:

```
Decimal: 100, -45, 321
Hexadecimal (prefixed by 0x): 0x1F, 0xA5
Binary (prefixed by 0b): 0b1010, 0b1101
Octal (prefixed by 0): 012, 071
Floating-Point Literals:

```

```
Decimal form: 3.14, 0.001, -45.67
Exponential form: 1.23e3 (equivalent to 1.23 *
 10^3),
5.67e-2 (equivalent to 5.67 * 10^-2)
```

Using Numbers in Java Code: In Java, numbers are used in calculations, assignments, and expressions. You can directly assign numeric literals to variables of the appropriate type. Here are some examples:

```java
// Integer examples
int age = 25;
// Using 'L' suffix for long literal:
long population = 7800000000L;

// Floating-point examples
double pi = 3.14159;
float g = 9.8F; // Using 'F' suffix for float
literal

// Hexadecimal, binary, and octal literals
int hexValue = 0x1A; // 26 in decimal
int binaryValue = 0b1011; // 11 in decimal
int octalValue = 012; // 10 in decimal
```

Working with Large Numbers Java allows underscores in numeric literals to make large numbers more readable. For instance:

```java
// Easier to read than 1000000:
int largeNumber = 1_000_000;
```

```
long veryLargeNumber = 7_800_000_000L;
```

These underscores are ignored by the compiler and purely aid readability.

4.3 Exercises:

Identify Valid Identifiers: For each identifier below, determine if it's valid or invalid. If it's invalid, explain why:

```
userCount
2ndPlace
MAX_SCORE
final
product\$Price
```

Solution:

```
userCount - Valid
2ndPlace - Invalid (cannot start with a digit)
MAX_SCORE - Valid
final - Invalid (reserved keyword)
product\$Price - Valid
```

Identify Data Types: For each value below, state which Java data type it belongs to:

```
127
0.001F
123456789L
0x7B
```

```
5.67e2
```

Solution:

```
127 - byte or int
0.001F - float
123456789L - long
0x7B - int (hexadecimal for 123)
5.67e2 - double (scientific notation)
```

Write a Literal Expression: Write an expression using underscores to represent the number 1000000 for better readability. Solution:

```
int readableMillion = 1_000_000;
```

Define and Initialize Variables: Define and initialize variables in Java for each description below:

An integer variable height with a value of 180. A floating-point variable gravity with a value of 9.8. A long integer variable worldPopulation with a value of 7800000000. A hexadecimal integer variable colorCode with a value of 0xFF00FF. Solution:

```
int height = 180;
float gravity = 9.8F;
long worldPopulation = 7_800_000_000L;
int colorCode = 0xFF00FF;
```

Binary, Octal, and Hexadecimal Conversion: Convert the following values to their respective forms:

Binary 0b1101 to Decimal. Octal 077 to Decimal. Hexadecimal 0x2A to Decimal. Solution:

Binary 0b1101 = 13 in Decimal. Octal 077 = 63 in Decimal. Hexadecimal 0x2A = 42 in Decimal.

This chapter has introduced identifiers and numbers in Java. Practice these exercises to reinforce your understanding, and get ready for the next chapter, where we'll explore data types in depth!

Chapter 5

Data Description

In Java, data description defines the types and forms of data that a program can work with. This chapter will cover data types, the concept of constants and variables, typified programming languages, and the rules around identifiers.

5.1 Data Types

Data types specify the kind of values that can be stored in variables. In Java, data types are divided into two main categories:

Primitive Data Types: These are the basic types provided by Java for handling raw values. They are predefined by the language and include:

Integer Types: byte, short, int, and long, which store whole numbers. **Floating-Point Types**: float and double, which store decimal values. **Character Type**: char, which stores single characters like 'A' or '1'. **Boolean Type**: boolean, which represents true/false values.

Reference Data Types: These are objects or instances of classes and can store a much larger range of values. Common reference types include:

Strings: Text sequences, like "Hello, World!". **Arrays**: A collection of values of the same data type. **Classes and Interfaces**: Custom data types that store data and behavior. Each data type has a specific size and range, making it important to choose the right type based on the data you need to store.

5.2 Typified Programming Languages

Java is a strongly typed language, meaning that every variable and expression has a specific data type determined at compile time. This characteristic provides several benefits:

Type Safety: Prevents operations between incompatible types, reducing runtime errors. **Memory Efficiency**: Allocates the correct amount of memory for each variable. **Predictability**: Ensures that each variable behaves consistently according to its data type.

5.3 Constants

Constants are values that do not change once defined. In Java, constants are usually declared using the **final** keyword. Defining constants helps avoid accidental modification of critical values and enhances code readability.

Declaring Constants To declare a constant in Java, use the final keyword:

```
final double PI = 3.14159;
final int MAX_USERS = 100;
```

Constants are often written in uppercase to distinguish them from variables.

5.4 Variables

Variables are named storage locations that can hold data values. Unlike constants, the values of variables can be changed throughout the program. In Java, variables must be declared with a data type before they are used.

Declaring Variables To declare a variable, specify its data type, followed by the variable name:

```
int age;
double salary;
boolean isActive;
```

Variables can also be initialized at the time of declaration:

```java
int age = 30;
double salary = 55000.0;
boolean isActive = true;
```

5.5 Uniqueness of Identifiers

In Java, every identifier (name for a variable, constant, class, method, etc.) within the same scope must be unique. This rule prevents ambiguity and ensures that each identifier references a distinct entity.

Scopes and Uniqueness An identifier's scope is the part of the program where the identifier is valid. Scopes can be nested, and identifiers declared in an outer scope cannot be redefined in that scope but can be in an inner scope.

For example:

```java
int count = 10; // Outer scope

if (count > 5) {
    int innerCount = 20; // Inner scope
    // 'innerCount' is unique within this
    scope
}

// 'count' is still valid here
```

5.6 Exercises:

To help solidify your understanding, here are a few exercises.

Identify the Data Types: Identify the data type for each variable:

```
final double TAX_RATE = 0.2;
String name = "Alice";
boolean isOpen = true;
char grade = 'A';
```

Solution:

```
final double TAX_RATE = 0.2; - double
String name = "Alice"; - String (reference type)
boolean isOpen = true; - boolean
char grade = 'A'; - char
```

Constant Declaration:
Declare a constant for the speed of light, 299792458 meters per second, in Java.

Solution:

```
final int SPEED_OF_LIGHT = 299792458;
```

Variable Initialization: Declare and initialize variables for each scenario:

An integer maxAttempts with a value of 5. A double interestRate with a value of 4.5. A boolean isVerified with a value of false. Solution: int maxAttempts = 5; double interestRate = 4.5; boolean isVerified = false;

Uniqueness of Identifiers: Explain why the following code snippet is invalid:

```
int value = 100;
int value = 200;
```

Solution: This code is invalid because value is declared twice within the same scope, which violates the rule of unique identifiers within a scope.

This chapter has covered the fundamental concepts of data description in Java, setting up a solid foundation for understanding how to store and manage data in your programs. The next chapter will dive deeper into data manipulation and variable usage within Java programs.

Chapter 6

Action Description

In Java, an **action description** specifies the operations or tasks to be executed by the program. This chapter introduces different types of statements, expressions, operators, and input/output operations, as well as conditional statements like `if-then-else`.

6.1 Statement Part

The **statement part** in a Java program contains commands that are executed in sequence. Java statements are usually organized within methods, classes, and blocks. Each statement performs a specific action, such as variable assignment, output display, or control flow.

6.2 Assignment Statements

An **assignment statement** is used to assign a value to a variable. The assignment operator (=) assigns the value on the right-hand side to the variable on the left-hand side.

```
int number = 10; // assigns 10 to variable '
number'
double price = 19.99;
boolean isAvailable = true;
```

6.3 Compound Statements

Compound statements consist of multiple individual statements grouped together within curly braces {}. A compound statement is also known as a **block**.

```
{
    int x = 5;
    int y = x + 10;
    System.out.println(y);
}
```

Compound statements allow multiple lines of code to be treated as a single unit, which is essential in control structures like loops and conditionals.

6.4 Expressions

An **expression** is a combination of variables, constants, and operators that evaluates to a single value. Expressions are used in various parts of a Java program, including assignments, method calls, and control statements.

6.4.1 Types of Expressions

- **Arithmetic Expressions**: Perform mathematical calculations, e.g., `5 + 3`, `a - b`, `num * 2`.
- **Logical Expressions**: Use logical operators to produce a boolean result, e.g., `isAvailable && isOpen`, `!isActive`.
- **Boolean Expressions:** Compare two values and produce a boolean result, e.g., `x > 5`, `y == z`, `a != b`.

6.5 Operators and Their Priorities

Java has several types of operators, each with a specific purpose and precedence. **Operator precedence** determines the order in which operations are performed.

- **Operator:** `*`, `/`, `%`
  Description: Multiplication, Division, Modulus
  Example: `5 * 3`, `10 / 2`, `10 % 3`

- **Operator:** `+`, `-`
  Description: Addition, Subtraction
  Example: `5 + 2`, `x - y`

- **Operator:** `==`, `!=`, `>`, `<`, `>=`, `<=`
  Description: Comparison
  Example: `x == 10`, `y != 5`

- **Operator:** `&&`, `||`, `!`
  Description: Logical AND, OR, NOT
  Example: `a && b`, `!c`

- **Operator:** `=`
  Description: Assignment
  Example: `num = 10`

Operators with higher precedence (like `*`, `/`, `%`) are evaluated before lower precedence operators (like `+`, `-`). Parentheses can be used to control the order of evaluation in complex expressions.

```
// Parentheses force addition before multiplication
int result = (5 + 3) * 2;
```

6.6 Type Customization (Type Casting)

Type customization, or **type casting**, is the conversion of one data type to another. Java supports two types of casting:

- **Implicit Casting**: Automatically converts smaller types to larger compatible types.

```
int a = 10;
// Implicitly converts ‘a‘ to double:
double b = a;
```

- **Explicit Casting**: Manually converts one type to another using parentheses.

```
double value = 9.7;
// Explicitly casts ‘value‘ to int:
int intValue = (int) value;
```

6.7 Standard Input and Output (write/read)

Java provides built-in methods for reading input and writing output.

6.7.1 Writing Output

The `System.out.print()` and `System.out.println()` methods display text on the console.

- `System.out.print()`: Prints text without a newline.
- `System.out.println()`: Prints text followed by a newline.

```
System.out.print("Hello ");
System.out.println("World!");
// Output: Hello World!
```

6.7.2 Reading Input

To read input, Java uses the `Scanner` class, which reads input from the console.

```
import java.util.Scanner;

Scanner scanner = new Scanner(System.in);
System.out.print("Enter a number: ");
int number = scanner.nextInt(); // Reads an integer
System.out.println("You entered: " + number);
```

6.8 The `if-then-else` Conditional Statement

The `if-then-else` statement is a control structure that executes a block of code if a specified condition is true and optionally executes another block if the condition is false.

```
if (condition) {
    // code to execute if condition is true
} else {
    // code to execute if condition is false
}
```

Example:

```
int age = 20;

if (age >= 18) {
    System.out.println("You are an adult.");
} else {
    System.out.println("You are a minor.");
}
```

Exercises

1. **Simple Assignment**
   Declare an integer variable `score` and assign it the value `85`.

```java
int score = 85;
```

2. **Expression Evaluation**
   Calculate the result of the following expression in Java: `(5 + 3) * 2 - 10 / 2`.

```java
int result = (5 + 3) * 2 - 10 / 2;
// result = 11
```

3. **Operator Priority**
   Using parentheses, rewrite the following expression to force addition before division: `10 / 2 + 3`.

```java
int result = 10 / (2 + 3);
// result = 2
```

4. **Using `if-then-else`**
   Write an `if-then-else` statement to check if a variable `temperature` is above `30`. If true, print "Hot"; otherwise, print "Cold".

```java
int temperature = 25;

if (temperature > 30) {
    System.out.println("Hot");
} else {
    System.out.println("Cold");
}
```

5. **Standard Input**
   Write a small Java program that asks the user for their name and prints "Hello, [name]!" where `[name]` is the user's input.

```java
import java.util.Scanner;

public class GreetUser {
    public static void main(String[] args) {
    Scanner scanner = new Scanner(System.in);
        System.out.print("Enter your name: ");
        String name = scanner.nextLine();
    System.out.println("Hello, " + name + "!");
    }
}
```

This chapter introduces the essential components of action description in Java. With these foundations, you can begin creating dynamic programs that respond to user input, perform calculations, and control the flow of execution based on conditions. Practice these exercises to reinforce your understanding before moving to more advanced topics.

6.9 User-Defined Types

Introduction to User-Defined Types

In Java, user-defined types allow programmers to create more complex data structures by extending standard types. This chapter covers three major categories of user-defined types: structured types, pointer types, and simple types, including enumerated and subrange types.

User-defined types enable us to model data in ways that closely match real-world concepts. This flexibility is essential for structuring complex programs and efficiently organizing data.

6.9.1 Structured Types

Structured types allow multiple data elements to be grouped together into a single type. In Java, structured types include classes and arrays, which can hold both primitive and other user-defined types.

Classes

Classes are versatile structured types in Java. A class groups fields (variables) and methods (functions) together, creating an object blueprint. Each instance of a class (object) has its own copies of fields, allowing for multiple objects with similar but independent data.

```
class Person {
    String name;
    int age;
```

```java

    public Person(String name, int age) {
        this.name = name;
        this.age = age;
    }

    public void displayInfo() {
    System.out.println("Name:"+ name+ ", Age:"
     + age);
    }
}
```

In this example, the `Person` class has fields `name` and `age` and a method `displayInfo()` to output information about a person.

Arrays

An array is a collection of elements of the same type stored in contiguous memory. Arrays in Java are fixed in size and are zero-indexed.

```java
int[] numbers = {1, 2, 3, 4, 5};
System.out.println(numbers[2]); // Output: 3
```

Arrays are commonly used for grouping data of the same type, making them a fundamental part of structured types in Java.

6.9.2 Pointer Types

Java does not have explicit pointers as in languages like C or C++; however, references in Java can be understood as a safe form of pointer. When a variable stores an object, it holds a reference to that object's memory location rather than the actual data itself.

```
Person personA = new Person("Alice", 30);
// Both point to the same object:
Person personB = personA;
personB.age = 35;
System.out.println(personA.age);
// Output: 35
```

In this example, `personA` and `personB` both reference the same object in memory. Thus, changing the object through one reference affects the other.

6.9.3 Simple Types

Simple user-defined types are restricted to a specific set of values or range. This section introduces enumerated types and subrange types.

Enumerated Types

An **enumerated type** is a special data type that consists of a fixed set of constants. Enumerated types are useful when a variable should only hold a restricted set of values. In Java, they are defined using the `enum` keyword.

```java
enum Day {
MONDAY,TUESDAY,WEDNESDAY,THURSDAY,FRIDAY,
SATURDAY,SUNDAY
}

Day today = Day.MONDAY;
```

Enumerated types make code more readable and maintainable by providing a fixed set of valid values.

Subrange Types

A **subrange type** is a subset of an existing type. Although Java does not natively support subranges, we can simulate them by limiting the values assigned to a variable. For example, a month can only be between 1 and 12:

```java
int month = 5; // Valid month

if (month >= 1 && month <= 12) {
    System.out.println("Month is valid.");
} else {
    System.out.println("Month is invalid.");
}
```

Subrange types ensure that values are within a specific range, helping to prevent errors from out-of-range values.

6.9.4 Exercises

1. **Class Definition** Define a class Book with fields for title, author, and publication year. Create a constructor and a method to display the book information.

```
class Book {
        String title;
        String author;
        int year;

public Book(String title, String author,
int year) {
            this.title = title;
            this.author = author;
            this.year = year;
        }

public void displayBookInfo() {
System.out.println(
"Title:"+title+",Author:"+author+",Year:"+
year);
        }
    }
```

2. **Array Usage** Create an array of integers with five elements, assign values to each, and print the sum of all elements.

```
    int[] numbers = {5, 10, 15, 20, 25};
```

```
    int sum = 0;

    for (int num : numbers) {
        sum += num;
    }

    System.out.println("Sum: " + sum);
    // Output: Sum: 75
```

3. **Enum Declaration** Define an enumerated type for seasons (Spring, Summer, Fall, Winter). Then, declare a variable of this type and assign it a value.

```
    enum Season {
        SPRING, SUMMER, FALL, WINTER
    }

    Season currentSeason =
    Season.SUMMER;
    System.out.println("Current season:"
    +currentSeason);
```

4. **Subrange Emulation** Write code to check if an integer variable `score` is between 0 and 100. Print "Valid score" if it is within range and "Invalid score" otherwise.

```
    int score = 85;

    if (score >= 0 && score <= 100) {
```

```
        System.out.println("Valid score.")
        ;
    } else {
        System.out.println("Invalid score.
        ");
    }
```

With these exercises, you should now have a solid foundation in user-defined types. From structured types like classes and arrays to enumerated and subrange types, these tools enable more precise and organized data management in Java programs.

Chapter 7

Loops in Java

Loops are a fundamental aspect of programming, allowing us to repeat a block of code multiple times. Java provides several types of loops, each suited to different needs. This chapter will cover the `for` loop, `while` loop, `do-while` loop, and enhanced `for` loop, giving you a solid foundation for managing repetitive tasks in Java.

7.1 The `for` Loop

The `for` loop is ideal when you know how many times you want to execute a statement or a block of code. A typical `for` loop includes an initialization, a condition, and an increment/decrement step.

Syntax:

```
for (initialization; condition; increment/
decrement) {
```

```
    // Code to execute in each loop iteration
}
```

Example:

```
for (int i = 0; i < 5; i++) {
    System.out.println("Iteration: " + i);
}
```

In this example, i starts at 0, increments by 1 in each loop, and stops when it reaches 5.

7.2 The while Loop

The `while` loop executes a block of code as long as a specified condition is `true`. It's especially useful when you don't know beforehand how many times the loop should run, as it depends on dynamic conditions determined at runtime.

Syntax:

```
while (condition) {
    // Code to execute as long as condition is
      true
}
```

Example:

```
import java.util.Scanner;

Scanner scanner = new Scanner(System.in);
int input;
```

```

System.out.println("Enter a number greater than 10:");

while ((input = scanner.nextInt()) <= 10) {
    System.out.println("Try again.
    Enter a number greater than 10:");
}

System.out.println("Thank you! You entered: " + input);
```

In this example, the loop depends on the user's input, and we don't know beforehand how many times it will run, as it repeats until the user enters a number greater than 10.

7.3 The `do-while` Loop

The `do-while` loop is similar to the `while` loop, but with one key difference: it guarantees the code executes at least once, regardless of the condition, since the condition is checked after the code block.

Syntax:

```
do {
    // Code to execute at least once
} while (condition);
```

Example:

```
int i = 5;
do {
    System.out.println("Iteration: " + i);
    i--;
} while (i > 0);
```

Even if `i` were initialized to a value greater than 5, this loop would execute once before checking the condition.

7.4 Enhanced `for` Loop (for-each Loop)

Java also provides an enhanced `for` loop, or for-each loop, primarily for iterating over arrays or collections. It's convenient when you don't need access to the index and only care about each element in the collection.

Syntax:

```
for (Type item : collection) {
    // Code to execute with each item
}
```

Example:

```
int[] numbers = {1, 2, 3, 4, 5};
for (int number : numbers) {
    System.out.println("Number: " + number);
}
```

This loop iterates over each element in the `numbers` array and prints it.

7.5 Nested Loops

Loops can also be nested, meaning one loop inside another. Nested loops are useful when working with multi-dimensional data, such as matrices.

Example:

```
for (int i = 1; i <= 3; i++) {
    for (int j = 1; j <= 3; j++) {
        System.out.println("i: " + i + ", j: "
        + j);
    }
}
```

In this case, for every iteration of `i`, the inner loop completes all its iterations of `j`.

7.6 Exercises

1. **Using a `for` Loop**
   Write a `for` loop that prints all even numbers between 1 and 10.

   Solution:

   ```
       for (int i = 2; i <= 10; i += 2) {
           System.out.println(i);
       }
   ```

2. **Using a `while` Loop**
   Write a `while` loop that prints numbers from 1 to

5.

Solution:

```
int i = 1;
while (i <= 5) {
    System.out.println(i);
    i++;
}
```

3. **Using a `do-while` Loop**
   Use a `do-while` loop to print the numbers from 5 down to 1.

   Solution:

```
int i = 5;
do {
    System.out.println(i);
    i--;
} while (i > 0);
```

4. **Using an Enhanced `for` Loop**
   Create an array of strings with names of the days of the week. Use an enhanced `for` loop to print each day.

   Solution:

```
String[] days =
{"Monday","Tuesday","Wednesday",
"Thursday","Friday","Saturday","Sunday
"};
```

```
    for (String day : days) {
        System.out.println(day);
    }
```

Chapter 8

Structured Types in Java

Structured data types allow us to group related elements, enhancing program organization and efficiency. This chapter covers arrays (single and multidimensional), records (as a way of structuring data with classes), indexed variables, and strings.

Arrays in Java

An array is a collection of elements of the same data type, stored in contiguous memory locations, allowing efficient access to each element.

Declaring and Initializing Arrays

To declare an array, specify the data type and use square brackets `[]`. Here's the basic syntax for declaring and initializing an array:

```java
// Declaration
int[] numbers;

// Initialization
numbers = new int[5];

// Declaration and initialization
int[] numbers = {1, 2, 3, 4, 5};
```

In the example above, `numbers` can hold 5 integers, accessed by index (starting from 0).

Accessing Array Elements

Array elements are accessed with an index. For example:

```java
System.out.println(numbers[0]);
// Accesses the first element (1)
```

Multidimensional Arrays

Java supports multidimensional arrays, useful for representing tables or matrices. Each additional dimension is represented with extra square brackets.

```java
int[][] matrix = {
    {1, 2, 3},
    {4, 5, 6},
    {7, 8, 9}
};
System.out.println(matrix[1][2]);
// Accesses the element 6
```

In this example, `matrix` is a 3x3 array, and we access the element in the second row and third column using `matrix[1][2]`.

Exercises with Solutions

Exercise 1: Single-dimensional array

Write a Java program that creates an array of 10 integers, initializes it with numbers 1 through 10, and prints each element.

```java
public class SingleDimArrayExample {
    public static void main(String[] args) {
        int[] numbers =
        {1, 2, 3, 4, 5, 6, 7, 8, 9, 10};
        for (int i = 0; i < numbers.length; i
        ++) {
            System.out.println(
            "Element at index " + i + ": "
            + numbers[i]);
        }
```

```
    }
}
```

Exercise 2: Two-dimensional array

Write a Java program to create a 2x3 array of doubles, initialize it, and print each element.

```
public class TwoDimArrayExample {
    public static void main(String[] args) {
        double[][] matrix = {
            {1.1, 2.2, 3.3},
            {4.4, 5.5, 6.6}
        };
        for (int i = 0; i < matrix.length; i++)
         {
        for (
        int j = 0; j < matrix[i].length; j++) {
            System.out.println(
            "Element at [" + i + "][" + j + "]:
             "
            + matrix[i][j]);
            }
        }
    }
}
```

Records Using Classes

Java's class structure can be used to group different types of related data together. Here's an example of a `Person` class.

```
class Person {
    String name;
    int age;

    Person(String name, int age) {
        this.name = name;
        this.age = age;
    }

    void display() {
        System.out.println("Name: " + name + ", Age: " + age);
    }
}
```

Using this class, we can create multiple `Person` objects.

Solution Example

```
public class PersonExample {
    public static void main(String[] args) {
        Person person1 = new Person("Alice", 25);
```

```java
        Person person2 = new Person("Bob", 30);

        person1.display();
        person2.display();
    }
}
```

Using Records in Java (Java 16 and Later)

With Java 16 and later, you can create records, which simplify creating data-holding structures.

```java
record Person(String name, int age) {}
```

Exercise:

Create a **Person** *class or record that includes fields for a person's name and age. Create two instances and display their information.*

```java
public class PersonExercise {
    public static void main(String[] args) {
        Person person1 = new Person("Alice",
        22);
        Person person2 = new Person("John", 28)
        ;

        System.out.println(person1);
        System.out.println(person2);
    }
```

```
}
```

Component Types, Index Types, and Indexed Variables

Arrays consist of a component type, the type of elements stored. For example, in `int[]`, the component type is `int`. Array indices in Java are integers starting from 0, and each element is an *indexed variable.*

Example with Solution

```
public class ArrayExample {
    public static void main(String[] args) {
        String[] names = {"Alice", "Bob", "
        Charlie"};
        for (int i = 0; i < names.length; i++)
        {
            System.out.println(
            "Name at index " + i + ": " + names
            [i]);
        }
    }
}
```

Exercise:

Create an array of `double` *values representing temperatures over a week. Calculate and print the average temperature.*

```
public class TemperatureExample {
    public static void main(String[] args) {
        double[] temperatures =
        {72.5, 75.0, 78.3, 80.0, 77.4, 73.5,
        76.2};
        double sum = 0.0;
        for (double temp : temperatures) {
            sum += temp;
        }
        double average = sum / temperatures.
        length;
        System.out.println(
        "Average temperature: " + average);
    }
}
```

Strings in Java

Strings are sequences of characters and are immutable. Java offers many methods to manipulate strings.

Creating and Using Strings

```
String greeting = "Hello, World!";
String name = new String("Alice");
```

Common String Operations

Concatenation

```
String fullName = "John" + " " + "Doe";
```

Length

```
int length = greeting.length();
```

Substring

```
String sub = greeting.substring(0, 5); // "
Hello"
```

Comparison

```
boolean isEqual = greeting.equals("Hello,
World!");
```

Exercise:

Write a Java program that takes a user's full name as input, splits it into first and last names, and prints each part.

```
import java.util.Scanner;

public class StringExample {
    public static void main(String[] args) {
```

```
        Scanner scanner = new Scanner(System.in);
        System.out.print("Enter your full name: ");
        String fullName = scanner.nextLine();

        String[] nameParts = fullName.split(" ");
        System.out.println("First name:"
        + nameParts[0]);
        if (nameParts.length > 1) {
            System.out.println("Last name: "
            + nameParts[nameParts.length - 1]);
        }
        scanner.close();
    }
}
```

Summary

This chapter introduced structured data types, including:

- **Arrays**: for managing collections of data.
- **Records (using classes)**: for grouping related data fields.
- **Strings**: for handling sequences of characters with useful built-in operations.

By now, you should understand how to create and work with these types.

Chapter 9

Understanding References and Memory in Java

Java manages data in two main types of memory: the **stack** and the **heap**. This chapter will explain the concepts of **primitive data types** and **reference types**—and how Java uses **references** to store and manipulate data in memory.

9.1 Primitive vs. Reference Types

In Java, variables are divided into two primary categories:

- **Primitive Types**: These store basic data values directly in memory. Primitive types include `int`, `double`, `char`, and `boolean`.

- **Reference Types**: These store references (or "addresses") to data stored elsewhere in memory, specifically in the heap. Variables that store data structures like `String` or arrays are reference types.

9.1.1 Example: Primitive vs. Reference Types

Consider the following code:

```java
int x = 10;                    // Primitive type
String greeting = "Hello"; // Reference type
```

Here, `x` is a primitive variable that directly stores the integer value `10` in the stack. `greeting` is a reference variable; it doesn't store the `String` data itself but rather a reference to it, meaning an address in memory where `"Hello"` is stored in the heap.

9.2 Memory Model: Stack and Heap

In Java:

- The **stack** is used to store local variables and method calls.

- The **heap** stores data structures that need to be accessible beyond the immediate scope of a single method.

9.2.1 How the Stack and Heap Work Together

Consider this example:

```
int a = 5;
String city = "Paris";
```

- `a` is a primitive type, so `5` is stored directly on the stack.
- `city` is a reference type, so the stack holds a reference to `"Paris"`, which is stored in the heap.

When methods are called, local variables are pushed to the stack, and when they return, those variables are popped off. However, data stored in the heap persists until it is no longer referenced and becomes eligible for **garbage collection**.

9.3 Assigning Reference Variables

Assigning one reference variable to another does not create a new copy of the data but instead copies the reference, so both variables then point to the same data in the heap.

9.3.1 Example: Reference Assignment

```
String city1 = "Paris";
String city2 = city1;
city2 = "Berlin";
```

In this case:

- Initially, both `city1` and `city2` refer to the `"Paris"` data.
- When `city2` is reassigned to `"Berlin"`, only `city2` changes its reference. `city1` still points to `"Paris"`.

9.4 Null References, NullPointerException

In Java, a reference variable can point to **null**, meaning it doesn't reference any data. Using a `null` reference without checking can cause a `NullPointerException`.

9.4.1 Example: Null Reference

```
String language = null;
System.out.println(language.length());
// Causes NullPointerException
```

In this code, attempting to access `language.length()` when `language` is null throws an exception since there's no actual data to access.

9.4.2 Exercise 1: Understanding Null References

Declare a reference variable for an array, set it to null, and attempt to access an element. What error do you get?

Solution:

```
int[] numbers = null;
//Next line Causes NullPointerException:
System.out.println(numbers[0]);
```

This will cause a `NullPointerException` because `numbers` doesn't point to an actual array in memory.

9.5 Garbage Collection

Java includes an automatic **garbage collector** that reclaims memory from data no longer referenced. This helps manage memory by cleaning up data that can no longer be accessed.

9.6 Pass-By-Value in Java

Java uses **pass-by-value** for all variables, whether primitive or reference types. This means that when a method is called, a copy of the variable's value is passed.

- For primitive types, this is straightforward: the actual value is passed.

- For reference types, the value of the reference is copied, so both the original and copied references point to the same data in the heap.

9.6.1 Example: Pass-By-Value with References

```java
public class Example {
    public static void modifyArray(int[] data)
     {
        data[0] = 99;
    }

    public static void main(String[] args) {
        int[] numbers = {1, 2, 3};
        modifyArray(numbers);
        System.out.println(numbers[0]); //
        Outputs: 99
    }
}
```

In this code, `numbers` and `data` refer to the same array in memory, so modifications inside `modifyArray` affect the original array.

9.6.2 Exercises and Solutions

Exercise 2: Understanding References and the Heap

Create a method that takes an array as a parameter, modifies it, and observe the changes in the calling code.

Solution:

```
public class ReferenceExample {
    public static void changeArray(int[] array) {
        array[0] = 99;
    }

    public static void main(String[] args) {
        int[] numbers = {1, 2, 3};
        changeArray(numbers);
        System.out.println(numbers[0]); // Outputs: 99
    }
}
```

In this example, `changeArray` modifies the `numbers` array. Since `numbers` and `array` refer to the same data in memory, changes in `changeArray` are reflected in `numbers`.

Exercise 3: Testing Pass-By-Value

Write a method that takes a `String` parameter, modifies it, and observe the result.

Solution:

```
public class PassByValue {
    public static void modifyString(String text) {
        text = "Modified";
    }

    public static void main(String[] args) {
        String original = "Original";
        modifyString(original);
        System.out.println(original);
        // Outputs: "Original"
    }
}
```

Since `String` is immutable and Java uses pass-by-value, the modification within `modifyString` has no effect on `original`.

9.7 A Note on Future Topics

The concept of reference types will be very important when we start working with **objects**. While we're focusing on simpler reference types like arrays and `String` for now, this concept extends to more complex data structures in Java. In future chapters, we'll build on this understanding to explain how Java uses references to handle objects in object-oriented programming.

—

This chapter on references and memory provides a foundation for understanding how Java manages data, setting the stage for working with objects and understanding the memory implications of object-oriented programming.

Chapter 10

Object-Oriented Concepts

The object-oriented paradigm is based on the concept of **objects**, entities that encapsulate data and behavior in a way that mirrors real-world items. This section will introduce the fundamental principles of objects in programming and the essential features of object-oriented programming (OOP).

10.1 The Worldview of Objects

In the world of object-oriented programming, **objects** are entities that exist independently and have unique **identities**, just like tangible items in the physical world. Each object is responsible for maintaining its **state** and can receive and react to messages from other objects or even from itself.

Objects have several key properties:

- **Identity**: Each object is a distinct entity, maintaining its own identity even when its state changes. An object, once created, remains the same unique object regardless of how it evolves over time.
- **State and Attributes**: An object's state is defined by its **attributes** (properties or fields). These attributes may include simple data, such as numbers or strings, or references to other objects, defining relationships and dependencies. Since an object's state can change, it is dynamic, allowing it to react to events and inputs over its lifetime.
- **Messages and Communication**: Objects interact by sending **messages** to each other. When an object receives a message, it decides how to react based on its own internal logic and state. The types of messages an object can respond to are determined by its attributes and abilities (methods). Messages serve as orders placed to an object, requesting it to perform an action or provide information. This separation between **order placement** (through messages) and **order execution** (through methods) is a central aspect of the object-oriented paradigm.
- **Lifetime**: Objects have a lifecycle—they are **created** (instantiated) and can be **destroyed** when no longer needed. The emergence and eventual

"passing away" of objects are natural processes in OOP, enabling dynamic, flexible systems.

- **Independence and Parallel Execution**: Objects are designed to act independently, operating as self-contained units. This allows them to function in parallel, much like independent entities in a system, each responsible for maintaining its own state and responding to messages as needed.

10.2 Relationships and State Changes

To interact with another object, an object must know of its existence, typically through a reference that is part of its state. Relationships between objects are formed based on the references they hold to one another, creating a network of dependencies and connections. Objects can also gain new connections by receiving references as parameters through messages. This structure of interconnected references allows objects to send and receive messages flexibly.

Objects' states are influenced not only by their attributes but also by the relationships they maintain with other objects. These relationships are a fundamental part of an object's identity and state.

10.3 Example: Objects and Message Passing

Imagine a simple system of two objects, `Printer` and `Document`. When a `Document` object wants to be printed, it sends a `print` message to the `Printer` object. The `Printer` object, upon receiving this message, reacts by executing its `print` method. The `Document` object only needs to know the `Printer` object by reference; it does not need to know how the printing is actually done—this is managed within the `Printer`'s own logic.

```java
public class Document {
    private Printer printer;

    public Document(Printer printer) {
        this.printer = printer;
    }

    public void sendToPrint() {
        printer.print(this);
    }
}

public class Printer {
    public void print(Document doc) {
        System.out.println("Printing document...");
    }
}
```

In this example, the `Document` object knows the `Printer` through a reference. When `sendToPrint()` is called on the `Document`, it sends a `print` message to the `Printer`. The separation of message placement and order execution is evident: `sendToPrint` places the order, and the `print` method on `Printer` executes it.

10.4 The Concept of State and Change

Objects are not static; they have the ability to change their state over time as they react to messages. This ability to respond and change is crucial in designing interactive, dynamic systems. For example, the `Document` object could change its status to "printed" after the `print` message is successfully processed by the `Printer`.

This worldview—where objects represent entities with unique identities, can change over time, send and receive messages, and execute tasks independently—forms the basis of object-oriented programming. With this foundation, we can now explore specific object-oriented features, such as encapsulation, inheritance, and polymorphism, which build on these core principles.

10.5 Message Sending and Attribute Change

In object-oriented programming, **message sending** enables objects to interact with one another by placing requests or orders. When an object sends a message, it essentially requests that another object execute a specific operation, often with the goal of producing a change in the receiving object's state.

Consider the following examples, which illustrate the different contexts in which message sending occurs:

10.5.1 Example 1: Requesting a Book from Any Library

Imagine `Bob` wants to borrow a specific book from a library. In this scenario, it does not matter which library he chooses, as long as it is capable of providing the book. Bob sends a `borrowBook` message to a `Library` object, which will then execute the request if it has the book in its collection. The choice of library is secondary, as the order itself is the primary concern.

```
public class Bob {
    public void borrowBook(Library library,
    String bookTitle) {
        library.borrowBook(bookTitle);
    }
}

```

```java
public class Library {
    public void borrowBook(String bookTitle) {
        System.out.println("Borrowing " +
        bookTitle);
    }
}
```

In this case, Bob's message to the library does not alter his personal state, nor does he require a specific library to execute the order. The focus is on the result of the action—the book is borrowed.

10.5.2 Example 2: Starting a Specific Motorcycle

Now consider that Bob wants to start his motorcycle. This action is different because it is specific to *his motorcycle*. Bob sends a `start` message to his motorcycle, which executes the request by invoking its `startEngine` method, changing the state of the motorcycle so that the engine is running. Here, Bob is concerned not with any arbitrary motorcycle, but specifically his own.

```java
public class Bob {
    private Motorcycle motorcycle;

    public Bob(Motorcycle motorcycle) {
        this.motorcycle = motorcycle;
    }

    public void startMotorcycle() {
```

```
        motorcycle.startEngine();
    }
}

public class Motorcycle {
    private boolean engineRunning = false;

    public void startEngine() {
        engineRunning = true;
        System.out.println("Engine is now
        running.");
    }
}
```

In this example, the message `startEngine()` initiates an action that modifies the state of the `Motorcycle` object, specifically changing the attribute `engineRunning` to `true`. This reflects a key concept in object-oriented programming: the **ability to execute orders resides in the methods of the receiving object**, while the **state or attributes of the object are stored in its variables**.

10.5.3 Local Variables as Attributes

The state of an object is generally maintained through its **local variables**, which represent its attributes. For example, in the `Motorcycle` class above, the `engineRunning` variable reflects whether the engine is on or off. When Bob sends the `startEngine` message, the `Motorcycle` object's method modifies this attribute, changing its state to reflect that the engine is now running.

In summary, message sending allows objects to communicate requests to each other. While some messages may be executed by any object with the proper capabilities (as with libraries), others are intended for a specific object, with the expectation that it will alter its unique state in response. This dynamic of sending messages and modifying attributes lies at the core of object-oriented design.

10.6 Classification and Inheritance

In object-oriented programming, **classification** and **inheritance** are essential concepts that help organize and structure code. These concepts allow us to create reusable, extensible systems by defining classes and their relationships.

Classes and Classification

A **class** is a blueprint for creating objects. Each class represents a specific type of object with common attributes (properties) and behaviors (methods). When we classify objects by grouping them into classes, we define general attributes and behaviors that apply to all objects of that class.

For example, in a program that manages animals, we might define a `Animal` class, and classify different kinds of animals (such as `Dog`, `Cat`, and `Bird`) as objects or instances of this class.

```
public abstract class Animal {
    public abstract void makeSound();
}

public class Dog extends Animal {
    @Override
    public void makeSound() {
        System.out.println("Woof!");
    }
}

public class Cat extends Animal {
    @Override
    public void makeSound() {
        System.out.println("Meow!");
    }
}
```

In this example, `Animal` is a general class that defines a `makeSound()` method. Specific classes, such as `Dog` and `Cat`, inherit from `Animal` and define their unique implementations of `makeSound()`.

Abstract Classes

An **abstract class** is a class that cannot be instantiated directly. Instead, it serves as a template for other classes, which inherit from it. Abstract classes often contain methods that must be implemented by subclasses. In our example, `Animal` is an abstract class because we cannot create an instance of `Animal` itself; only specific animal types (like `Dog` or `Cat`) can be instantiated.

Inheritance and Specialization

Inheritance allows a class to inherit attributes and methods from another class. The class that inherits is called the **subclass**, and the class it inherits from is the **superclass**. This relationship enables a subclass to reuse code from its superclass and extend it with additional attributes or behaviors.

For example, a `Dog` is a more specific type of `Animal`, so it inherits from `Animal` and provides a specialized implementation of the `makeSound()` method. This specialization enables each subclass to define its unique behavior while sharing common functionality defined in the superclass.

Exercises

The following exercise helps reinforce these concepts. Given a list of classes and messages, follow the steps to classify them into a hierarchy and analyze the structure.

Exercise:

You have the following classes and messages:

- Classes: `Animal`, `Mammal`, `Bird`, `Dog`, `Cat`, `Parrot` - Messages: `makeSound`, `fly`, `giveBirth`

1. Identify which classes can understand each message. - `makeSound`: All animals understand this message. - `fly`: Only birds can understand this message. - `giveBirth`: Only mammals understand this message.

2. Arrange the classes into a hierarchy.

Here's a possible hierarchy: - `Animal` - `Mammal` - `Dog` - `Cat` - `Bird` - `Parrot`

3. Assign each message to the highest possible class. - `makeSound` can be placed in `Animal`, as all animals understand this message. - `fly` can be placed in `Bird`, as only birds understand this message. - `giveBirth` can be placed in `Mammal`, as only mammals understand this message.

4. Determine which classes could be abstract. - `Animal`, `Mammal`, and `Bird` can all be abstract, as they represent general categories that might not be instantiated directly. Concrete subclasses (`Dog`, `Cat`, `Parrot`) represent specific types of animals that can be instantiated.

Observation: Abstract classes generally appear higher in the hierarchy, as they represent general classifications, while concrete classes are lower and represent specific instances.

5. Consider the impact of adding a new class. - Adding a new class, such as `Bat` (a mammal that can fly), could affect the hierarchy, as it would need to inherit both mammal and flying properties. In some cases, this might lead to refactoring the hierarchy or using interfaces to represent shared behaviors like `fly` across different

classes.

Solution Summary:

This exercise demonstrates how message passing, class hierarchies, and inheritance work together in object-oriented programming. Defining abstract classes higher in the hierarchy allows for a clean, organized structure, while specialized behaviors can be implemented in concrete subclasses. Adding a new class may sometimes require restructuring or reconsideration of how behaviors are inherited, especially when behaviors overlap across categories.

Chapter 11

Procedural vs. Object-Oriented Programming

11.1 Introduction

In this chapter, we explore the differences between procedural programming and object-oriented programming (OOP) from various perspectives. Each paradigm brings unique strengths and is suited for different types of tasks. The main areas of comparison include information modeling, structuring, encapsulation, extensibility, and parallelism.

11.2 Modeling and Processing Information

Procedural programming emphasizes a top-down approach, where tasks are broken down into smaller, sequential steps executed by functions. Data and functions are separate, meaning data is passed through functions for manipulation.

Object-oriented programming, however, models information as "objects" that represent both data and behaviors. Each object is an independent entity with its own state and methods, allowing it to interact with other objects through messages.

11.3 Programmer's Perspective

From the programmer's perspective, procedural programming involves writing functions that perform operations on data structures. Functions are treated as the primary unit of execution.

In OOP, programmers define classes and objects that encapsulate both data and behavior. Instead of passing data through functions, objects interact through method calls, allowing for a more modular approach to problem-solving.

11.4 Structuring and Data Encapsulation

Procedural programming often requires discipline to manage and restrict access to shared data. Global variables are frequently used, which can lead to unintentional side effects if functions modify the same data.

In OOP, encapsulation is a key principle where data and methods are bundled together within an object. Each object can protect its data from outside modification, only exposing what is necessary through public methods. This controlled access enhances modularity and simplifies debugging.

11.5 Extensibility

In procedural programming, adding new functionality often requires adding new functions or modifying existing ones, potentially affecting the whole system. Changes can lead to cascading updates that impact multiple functions.

OOP offers a more extensible model through inheritance and polymorphism. By defining new subclasses, new features can be added with minimal changes to the existing codebase. For example, adding a new type of account in a banking application can be done by creating a new class that inherits from the base `Account` class, leveraging shared functionality.

11.6 Assignment, Procedure Call vs Message Sending and Method Execution

In procedural programming, a function is called with parameters to execute a specific task. The function then returns a result.

In OOP, objects communicate by sending messages to each other. A method executes in response to a message, with the flexibility to determine the best way to handle it. This separation between order placement (message) and execution (method) is a hallmark of OOP.

11.7 Parallelism

Procedural programs typically execute sequentially unless parallelism is manually implemented. Tasks may be difficult to parallelize because functions and data structures are often tightly coupled.

OOP naturally supports parallelism, as objects operate independently. Each object can work on its tasks concurrently, making it easier to develop scalable and concurrent systems.

11.8 Exercises and Solutions

Exercise 1: Task and Data Identification

Design an online store where users can browse items, add them to a cart, and checkout. How would you approach this problem in both procedural and object-oriented programming?

- **Procedural Approach**:
  - **Functions**: **displayItems()**, **addToCart(item)**, **calculateTotal(cart)**, **checkout(cart)**
  - **Data Structures**: `cart` (list of items), **inventory** (list of items available)

  Procedural programming separates functions and data, manipulating data directly through function calls.

- **Object-Oriented Approach**:
  - **Classes**: `Item`, `Cart`, `User`
  - **Interactions**: `user.cart.addItem(item)`

  Objects represent entities, encapsulating both data and behavior for a more modular approach.

Exercise 2: Encapsulation and Independence

In a system where user data needs to be accessed and updated, how do procedural and OOP paradigms handle encapsulation?

Solution:

- **Procedural Approach**: Functions may access shared data, leading to potential side effects if not carefully managed.
- **OOP Approach**: Objects encapsulate their data and control access through methods, providing better data protection and modularity.

Exercise 3: Extensibility

In a banking application, how would each paradigm manage adding a new type of account?

Solution:

- **Procedural Approach**: Adding new functions may introduce dependencies and complexity.
- **OOP Approach**: New classes can inherit from a base `Account` class, making extensions modular and easier to maintain.

Exercise 4: Message Assignment in Hierarchies

Given the classes `Vehicle`, `Car`, `Bicycle`, `Motorcycle`, assign the messages `startEngine()`, `applyBrakes()`, `fuelUp()`, and `accelerate()`. Organize classes in an inheritance hierarchy.

Solution:

- **Hierarchy**:
  - **Superclass**: **Vehicle**
  - **Subclasses**: **Car**, **Motorcycle** (motorized), **Bicycle** (non-motorized)
- **Message Assignment**:
  - `applyBrakes()` and `accelerate()` for `Vehicle`
  - `startEngine()` and `fuelUp()` for motorized subclasses

Exercise 5: Impact of Additional Classes

What effect would adding a `HybridBike` have on the hierarchy?

Solution: A **HybridBike** could inherit or combine properties from both `Bicycle` and `Motorcycle`, demonstrating OOP's flexibility in extending classes.

—

This comparison highlights the strengths and ideal uses of procedural and object-oriented paradigms, aiding in choosing the best paradigm based on project requirements.

Chapter 12

Execution of a Java Program

The execution of a Java program involves several steps, from writing the code to running it. In this chapter, we break down the process to help you understand how a Java program works, focusing on beginners exploring object-oriented programming.

12.1 Writing and Structuring a Java Program

Every Java program begins with a class definition. The class may contain methods and attributes, but at least one class must include a special method called the `main` method. The `main` method serves as the entry point of the program, where the execution begins.

Here's an example of a simple Java program:

```
public class HelloWorld {
    public static void main(String[] args) {
        System.out.println("Hello, World!");
    }
}
```

Explanation:

- `public`: The `main` method is accessible from anywhere.
- `static`: It belongs to the class itself rather than any object.
- `void`: It doesn't return any value.
- `main`: The name of the method that the JVM looks for when starting the program.
- `String[] args`: Allows the program to accept command-line arguments.

12.2 Compilation and Bytecode

Java is a compiled language. When you write a program, the source code (written in `.java` files) is converted into an intermediate language called Bytecode using the Java Compiler (`javac`). Bytecode is stored in `.class` files.

Steps:

1. Write your code in a file with a `.java` extension.
2. Use the command `javac HelloWorld.java` to compile the code.
3. If successful, a `HelloWorld.class` file is generated.

12.3 Role of the Java Virtual Machine (JVM)

The JVM is responsible for executing the Bytecode. It acts as an interpreter between the Bytecode and the machine-specific code of your platform.

Key Responsibilities of the JVM:

- Loading and verifying Bytecode.
- Managing memory (e.g., stack and heap).
- Executing the Bytecode using the execution engine.

To run your program, use the command:

```
java HelloWorld
```

12.4 Class Methods and the main-Method

The `main` method is always **`static`**. This means it doesn't require an object to be invoked. When the program starts, the JVM directly calls the `main` method, beginning the program's execution.

You can call other static or instance methods from the `main` method. For instance:

```
public class Greeting {
    public static void main(String[] args) {
        greet();
    }

    public static void greet() {
        System.out.println("
        Welcome to Java Programming!");
    }
}
```

12.5 Execution Flow

1. The JVM searches for the `main` method in the specified class.
2. It executes the code inside `main`.
3. The program terminates after the last statement in `main` is executed unless an error occurs.

12.6 Command-Line Arguments

You can pass arguments to your program through the `String[] args` parameter in the `main` method. These arguments are provided when running the program.

Example:

```
public class CommandLineExample {
    public static void main(String[] args) {
        if (args.length > 0) {
            System.out.println("
            First argument: " + args[0]);
        } else {
            System.out.println("
            No arguments provided!");
        }
    }
}
```

Run this program as:

```
java CommandLineExample Hello
```

Output:

```
First argument: Hello
```

12.7 Debugging and Error Handling

Errors during compilation or runtime are part of programming. Java provides helpful error messages for debugging.

Types of Errors:

- **Compile-time errors**: Syntax issues like missing semicolons or incorrect method calls.

- **Runtime errors**: Issues during program execution, such as dividing by zero or accessing invalid array indices.

12.8 Exercises

Exercise 1

Write a Java program that prints your name. Compile and execute it.

Solution:

```
public class MyName {
    public static void main(String[] args) {
        System.out.println("My name is John Doe.");
    }
}
```

Exercise 1: Write a program that takes two numbers as command-line arguments and prints their sum.
Solution:

Solution:

```
public class SumTwoNumbers {
    public static void main(String[] args) {
        if (args.length == 2) {
            int num1 = Integer.parseInt(args[0]);
            int num2 = Integer.parseInt(args[1]);
```

```
            System.out.println("
            Sum: " + (num1 + num2));
        } else {
            System.out.println("
            Please provide two numbers.");
        }
    }
}
```

Exercise 2

Create a program with intentional syntax errors and observe the compiler's messages. Then, fix the errors.

Solution: This exercise is open-ended. Write code with intentional errors (e.g., miss a semicolon or use an undefined variable), and learn from the compiler's feedback.

This chapter lays the foundation for understanding the execution of Java programs and prepares you to explore more advanced topics.

Chapter 13

Handling Exceptions in Java

13.1 Introduction to Exceptions

In Java, an **exception** is an event that disrupts the normal flow of a program. Exceptions occur during the execution of a program and are often caused by conditions such as invalid user input, resource unavailability, or logical errors in the program.

Java provides mechanisms to handle exceptions, allowing the program to recover or terminate gracefully instead of crashing. Proper exception handling is crucial for building robust and reliable applications.

- **Normal termination** refers to the successful completion of a program without errors.

- **Abrupt termination** occurs when an unhandled exception interrupts the program execution.

For example, attempting to divide a number by zero will cause an **ArithmeticException**, terminating the program if unhandled.

13.2 Try-Statements

Java uses the **try-catch-finally** construct to handle exceptions. The **try** block contains code that might throw an exception. The **catch** block handles the exception. The **finally** block is optional and used for cleanup, like closing files or releasing resources. It executes regardless of whether an exception is thrown.

Example: Handling Division by Zero

```
public class ExceptionExample {
    public static void main(String[] args) {
        try {
        // This will throw an
        ArithmeticException:
            int result = 10 / 0;
        } catch (ArithmeticException e) {
            System.out.println("
            Error: Division by zero is not
            allowed.");
        } finally {
```

```
                System.out.println("Execution
                completed.");
        }
    }
}
```

13.3 Throwing Exceptions

Java allows you to explicitly throw exceptions using the `throw` statement. Exceptions can be built-in (e.g., `IOException`, `NullPointerException`) or custom-defined.

- **Checked Exceptions** (e.g., **IOException**) must be declared in the method signature with the `throws` keyword or handled with a **try-catch** block.
- **Unchecked Exceptions** (e.g., **ArithmeticException**) are not required to be explicitly handled.

Example: Throwing an Exception

```
public class ThrowExample {
    public static void main(String[] args) {
        int age = 15;
        try {
            checkAge(age);
        } catch (IllegalArgumentException e) {
            System.out.println("
```

```
            Caught exception: " + e.getMessage
            ());
        }
    }

    public static void checkAge(int age) {
        if (age < 18) {
            throw new IllegalArgumentException(
            "Age must be 18 or older.");
        }
        System.out.println("Access granted.");
    }
}
```

13.4 Exception Handling and Message Passing

Exception handling integrates seamlessly with object-oriented programming. Exceptions propagate through the **call stack**. If a method does not catch an exception, it passes it to the calling method. This continues until the exception is caught or the program terminates.

Example: Propagating Exceptions

```
public class PropagationExample {
    public static void main(String[] args) {
        try {
```

```
            riskyMethod();
        } catch (ArithmeticException e) {
            System.out.println("
            Caught in main: " + e.getMessage());

        }
    }

    public static void riskyMethod() {
        int result = 10 / 0; // Exception
        thrown here
    }
}
```

13.5 Custom Exceptions

You can create your own exception by extending the `Exception` class.

Example: Custom Exception

```
class InvalidInputException extends Exception
{
    public InvalidInputException(String
    message) {
        super(message);
    }
}
```

```java

public class CustomExceptionExample {
    public static void main(String[] args) {
        try {
            processInput(-5);
        } catch (InvalidInputException e) {
            System.out.println("Error: " +
            e.getMessage());
        }
    }

    public static void processInput(int input)
    throws InvalidInputException {
        if (input < 0) {
            throw new InvalidInputException("
            Input must be non-negative.");
        }
        System.out.println("Valid input: " +
        input);
    }
}
```

13.6 Best Practices

- Catch specific exceptions instead of using generic ones like `Exception`.
- Avoid empty `catch` blocks.

- Use `finally` for cleanup tasks, such as closing files or releasing memory.
- Leverage custom exceptions for meaningful error messages.
- Use exception chaining to preserve stack traces:

```
throw new Exception(
    "message",
    cause
);
```

13.7 Exercises

1. Write a program to handle division by zero using `try-catch`.
2. Implement a custom exception to handle invalid user input.
3. Write a program that uses `try-finally` to ensure a file is closed.

Solutions

1. **Handling Division by Zero**

```
    public class DivisionExercise {
        public static void main(String[]
        args) {
```

```
            try {
                int num = 10, den = 0;
                System.out.println(num / den);
            } catch (ArithmeticException e) {
                System.out.println("
                Cannot divide by zero.");
            }
        }
    }
```

2. **Custom Exception Example**

```
    class InvalidInputException extends Exception {
        public InvalidInputException(
        String message) {
            super(message);
        }
    }

    public class CustomExercise {
        public static void main(String[] args) {
            try {
                validateInput(-1);
            } catch (InvalidInputException e) {
```

```
                System.out.println("Error:
                " +
                e.getMessage());
            }
        }

        public static void validateInput(
        int input)
        throws InvalidInputException {
            if (input < 0) {
                throw new
                InvalidInputException("
                Input cannot be negative.")
                ;
            }
        }
    }
```

3. **Ensuring File Closure**

```
    import java.io.*;

    public class FileExercise {
        public static void main(String[]
        args) {
            try {
                BufferedReader reader =
                new BufferedReader(
                new FileReader("file.txt"))
                ;
```

```
                try {
                    System.out.println(
                    reader.readLine());
                } finally {
                    reader.close();
                    System.out.println("
                    File closed.");
                }
            } catch (IOException e) {
                System.out.println("File
                error: " +
                e.getMessage());
            }
        }
    }
```

Chapter 14

Constructors, `this` Object, and Formal Parameters

14.1 Introduction

In object-oriented programming, constructors, the `this` object, and formal parameters are fundamental to creating and managing objects. This chapter introduces these concepts to help you understand how objects are initialized, how they reference themselves, and how they interact with the inputs provided during their creation.

14.2 Constructors

A *constructor* is a special method used to initialize an object. When you create an object using the `new` keyword, the constructor is called automatically.

Key Points about Constructors

- A constructor has the same name as the class it belongs to.
- It does not have a return type (not even `void`).
- It can be overloaded, meaning a class can have multiple constructors with different parameter lists.

Example: A Basic Constructor

```
class Book {
    String title;
    String author;

    // Constructor
    public Book(String title, String author) {
        this.title = title;
        this.author = author;
    }
}
public class Main {
    public static void main(String[] args) {
```

```
        Book book = new Book("1984", "George
        Orwell");
        System.out.println(book.title +
        " by " + book.author);
    }
}
```

Explanation: The constructor initializes the `title` and `author` fields when a new `Book` object is created.

14.3 Overloading Constructors

A class can have multiple constructors with varying parameter lists to provide flexibility when creating objects.

Example: Overloaded Constructors

```
class Book {
    String title;
    String author;

    // Constructor with parameters
    public Book(String title, String author) {
        this.title = title;
        this.author = author;
    }

    // Constructor without parameters
    public Book() {
```

```
        this.title = "Unknown";
        this.author = "Unknown";
    }
}
public class Main {
    public static void main(String[] args) {
        Book book1 = new Book("1984", "George
        Orwell");
        Book book2 = new Book();
        System.out.println(book1.title + " by "
        + book1.author);
        System.out.println(book2.title + " by "
        + book2.author);
    }
}
```

14.4 Constructor Chaining

Constructor chaining occurs when one constructor calls another constructor within the same class. This is done using the `this` keyword.

Example: Constructor Chaining

```
class Book {
    String title;
    String author;

```

```
    // Constructor with parameters
    public Book(String title, String author) {
        this.title = title;
        this.author = author;
    }

    // Constructor calling another constructor
    public Book(String title) {
        this(title, "Unknown");
    }
}
public class Main {
    public static void main(String[] args) {
        Book book = new Book("Animal Farm");
        System.out.println(book.title + " by
        " + book.author);
    }
}
```

14.5 The this Object

The `this` object represents the current instance of the class. It is used to:

1. Resolve naming conflicts between instance variables and parameters.

2. Call another constructor in the same class (constructor chaining).

3. Pass the current object as a parameter to other methods.

Example: Using `this` to Resolve Name Conflicts

```
class Book {
    String title;

    public Book(String title) {
        this.title = title; // Resolving the conflict
    }
}
```

14.6 Formal Parameters

Formal parameters are variables defined in the method or constructor signature. They are placeholders for the actual values (arguments) passed during a method call or object creation.

Key Points

- They are local to the method or constructor.
- Their scope ends when the method or constructor finishes execution.

Example: Parameters in Constructors

```
class Book {
    String title;

    public Book(String title) {
    // Formal parameter 'title' is used here:
        this.title = title;
    }
}
```

14.7 Exercises

Exercise 1: Constructor Overloading

Write a `Person` class with overloaded constructors:

1. One constructor accepts `name` and `age`.
2. Another constructor accepts only `name` and sets `age` to `0` by default.
3. A default constructor sets both `name` and `age` to `"Unknown"` and `0`.
4. Test your class by creating objects with all three constructors.

Solution

```java
class Person {
    String name;
    int age;

    // Constructor with name and age
    public Person(String name, int age) {
        this.name = name;
        this.age = age;
    }

    // Constructor with name only
    public Person(String name) {
        this(name, 0); // Constructor chaining
    }

    // Default constructor
    public Person() {
        this("Unknown", 0); // Constructor chaining
    }
}
public class Main {
    public static void main(String[] args) {
        Person p1 = new Person("Alice", 30);
        Person p2 = new Person("Bob");
        Person p3 = new Person();
        System.out.println(p1.name + " is "
        + p1.age + " years old.");
        System.out.println(p2.name + " is "
```

```
            + p2.age + " years old.");
            System.out.println(p3.name + " is "
            + p3.age + " years old.");
    }
}
```

Exercise 2: Using `this` for Constructor Chaining

Modify the `Person` class to use constructor chaining for initializing default values.

Solution

(Refer to the constructor chaining in Exercise 1.)

Exercise 3: Formal Parameters

In a `Car` class, write a constructor that uses a parameter named `model` to initialize a field of the same name. Resolve the naming conflict using `this`.

Solution

```
class Car {
    String model;

    public Car(String model) {
    // Resolving naming conflict with 'this':
```

```
        this.model = model;
    }
}
public class Main {
    public static void main(String[] args) {
        Car car = new Car("Toyota");
        System.out.println("Car model: " + car.
        model);
    }
}
```

This chapter lays the groundwork for understanding object construction and communication in Java, providing a solid base to explore inheritance and other advanced topics.

Chapter 15

Inheritance and Specialization

15.1 Introduction to Inheritance

Inheritance allows the creation of new classes (subclasses) from existing ones (superclasses). Subclasses inherit the attributes and methods of their superclasses, enabling code reuse and the addition of new functionalities.

15.2 Subclassing and Specialization

A subclass is a specialized version of its superclass. It can:

- Add new methods and attributes.

- Override existing methods to provide specific behavior.

15.2.1 Example

```
// Superclass
class Animal {
    public void speak() {
        System.out.println("
        This animal makes a sound.");
    }
}

// Subclass
class Dog extends Animal {
    @Override
    public void speak() {
        System.out.println("The dog barks.");
    }
}
```

Output:

```
The dog barks.
```

15.3 Overriding and Subtyping

Overriding: Subclasses redefine methods of the superclass to provide specialized behavior.

Subtyping: Subclasses can be treated as their superclasses. This is a cornerstone of polymorphism.

15.3.1 Example

```
// Demonstrating Subtyping
class Main {
    public static void main(String[] args) {
        Animal animal = new Dog(); // Subtype
        animal.speak(); // Calls Dog's speak()
        method
    }
}
```

Output:

```
The dog barks.
```

15.4 Dynamic Dispatching

Dynamic dispatching determines the method to call at runtime based on the object's actual type, not the reference type. This is fundamental to achieving polymorphism.

15.4.1 Example

```
class Shape {
    public void draw() {
```

```
        System.out.println("Drawing a generic shape.");
    }
}

class Circle extends Shape {
    @Override
    public void draw() {
        System.out.println("Drawing a circle.");
    }
}

class Rectangle extends Shape {
    @Override
    public void draw() {
        System.out.println("Drawing a rectangle.");
    }
}

public class Main {
    public static void main(String[] args) {
        Shape[] shapes =
        { new Circle(), new Rectangle(), new Shape() };

        for (Shape shape : shapes) {
            shape.draw();
```

```
        }
    }
}
```

Output:

```
Drawing a circle.
Drawing a rectangle.
Drawing a generic shape.
```

15.5 Exercises

Exercise 1: Subclassing

Define a superclass `Vehicle` and two subclasses `Car` and `Bike`. Implement a method `move()` in each class that outputs a message describing how the vehicle moves. Test the method by creating instances of each subclass and calling `move()`.

Solution

```
// Superclass
class Vehicle {
    public void move() {
        System.out.println("This vehicle moves.
        ");
    }
}

```

```java
// Subclass 1
class Car extends Vehicle {
    @Override
    public void move() {
        System.out.println("The car drives.");
    }
}

// Subclass 2
class Bike extends Vehicle {
    @Override
    public void move() {
        System.out.println("The bike pedals.");
    }
}

public class Main {
    public static void main(String[] args) {
        Vehicle car = new Car();
        Vehicle bike = new Bike();
        car.move();
        bike.move();
    }
}
```

Output:

```
The car drives.
The bike pedals.
```

Exercise 2: Overriding and Polymorphism

Repeat the example provided earlier on dynamic dispatching, with the additional requirement of implementing a `Triangle` class as a subclass of `Shape`. Test the polymorphic behavior.

Solution

```java
// Superclass
class Shape {
    public void draw() {
        System.out.println("Drawing a generic shape.");
    }
}

// Subclasses
class Circle extends Shape {
    @Override
    public void draw() {
        System.out.println("Drawing a circle.");
    }
}

class Rectangle extends Shape {
    @Override
    public void draw() {
```

```java
        System.out.println("Drawing a rectangle.");
    }
}

class Triangle extends Shape {
    @Override
    public void draw() {
        System.out.println("Drawing a triangle.");
    }
}

public class Main {
    public static void main(String[] args) {
        Shape[] shapes =
        { new Circle(), new Rectangle(),
        new Triangle(), new Shape() };

        for (Shape shape : shapes) {
            shape.draw();
        }
    }
}
```

Output:

```
Drawing a circle.
Drawing a rectangle.
Drawing a triangle.
```

```
Drawing a generic shape.
```

Exercise 3: Abstract Classes

Given the `Shape` class from the previous exercise, refactor it to be an abstract class. Add an abstract method `calculateArea()`. Implement this method in the subclasses and test it by creating an array of `Shape` objects.

Solution

```
// Abstract Class
abstract class Shape {
    public abstract void calculateArea();

    public void draw() {
        System.out.println("Drawing a shape.");
    }
}

// Subclasses
class Circle extends Shape {
    private double radius = 5;

    @Override
    public void calculateArea() {
        System.out.println("
        Area of circle: " +
        (Math.PI * radius * radius));
    }
```

```java
}

class Rectangle extends Shape {
    private double width = 4;
    private double height = 3;

    @Override
    public void calculateArea() {
        System.out.println("Area of rectangle:
        "
        + (width * height));
    }
}

public class Main {
    public static void main(String[] args) {
        Shape[] shapes =
        { new Circle(), new Rectangle() };

        for (Shape shape : shapes) {
            shape.calculateArea();
        }
    }
}
```

Output:

```
Area of circle: 78.53981633974483
Area of rectangle: 12.0
```

This chapter introduced fundamental concepts of inheritance and specialization, which serve as a foundation for building more complex and reusable object-oriented systems.

Chapter 16

Object-Oriented Programming Languages

16.1 Introduction

Object-oriented programming (OOP) has become a dominant paradigm for modern software development. While all object-oriented programming languages share core principles, such as encapsulation, inheritance, and polymorphism, they also differ significantly in how they implement these principles and in the features they offer.

This chapter provides an overview of the commonalities and differences among various object-oriented languages, including communication mechanisms, object description, type systems, inheritance models, and advanced runtime features.

Commonalities Across Object-Oriented Languages

16.1.1 Synchronous Communication

All OOP languages rely on communication between objects. This typically happens through synchronous message passing, where an object sends a message (method call) to another object, expecting a response.

Example: Java

```
class Sender {
    public void sendMessage(
    Receiver receiver,
    String message) {
        receiver.receiveMessage(message);
    }
}

class Receiver {
    public void receiveMessage(String message)
     {
        System.out.println("Received: " +
        message);
    }
}

```

```
public class Main {
    public static void main(String[] args) {
        Receiver receiver = new Receiver();
        Sender sender = new Sender();
        sender.sendMessage(receiver, "Hello,
        World!");
    }
}
```

Output:

```
Received: Hello, World!
```

This synchronous communication model is the backbone of most OOP systems.

16.2 Key Differences Between Object-Oriented Languages

16.2.1 Object Description

Languages differ in how they describe and define objects.

- **Java:** Classes are the primary way to define objects. Java also supports interfaces to define object behavior without implementation.
- **Python:** Classes are used, but Python supports dynamic addition of attributes and methods to objects at runtime.

- **C++:** Objects are described through classes and structures. C++ allows fine-grained control over memory and behavior via access specifiers and constructors/destructors.

16.2.2 Reflection

Reflection allows programs to inspect and modify their structure at runtime.

- **Java:** Comprehensive reflection API through the `java.lang.reflect` package.
- **C#:** Offers robust reflection capabilities with type metadata available through the `System.Reflection` namespace.
- **Python:** Built-in functions like `getattr()` and `setattr()` make reflection extremely flexible.

16.2.3 Type Systems

- **Static Typing:** Languages like Java and C++ enforce strict type rules at compile time.
- **Dynamic Typing:** Python and JavaScript determine types at runtime, offering flexibility but requiring careful testing.

16.2.4 Inheritance and Specialization

Inheritance is implemented differently across languages:

- **Single Inheritance:** Java, for example, supports single inheritance for classes but allows multiple inheritance for interfaces.
- **Multiple Inheritance:** C++ supports multiple inheritance but introduces complexity in resolving method calls (e.g., the diamond problem).

16.2.5 Encapsulation and Structuring Constructs

The way data and methods are encapsulated and accessed varies:

- **C++:** Allows fine-grained access control with public, private, and protected specifiers.
- **Python:** Encourages a more open approach, relying on naming conventions (e.g., `_variable` for private attributes).

16.2.6 Dynamic Dispatching

Dynamic dispatching determines method calls at runtime based on the object's actual type. This is universal but implemented differently:

- **Java and C#:** Use virtual tables (vtables) for method resolution.
- **Python:** Employs a dynamic type system and method resolution order (MRO).

16.2.7 Advanced Features

Parallelism Support

- Java: Includes threads and concurrency utilities (e.g., **java.util.concurrent**).
- Python: Provides threads and asynchronous programming through `async` and `await`.
- C#: Offers tasks, threads, and parallel LINQ for concurrency.

Distribution Support

- Java: RMI (Remote Method Invocation) and frameworks like Spring.
- Python: Tools like `Pyro` and built-in networking libraries.
- C#: Supports remoting and distributed systems through WCF and gRPC.

Dynamic Loading and Runtime Changes

- Java: Allows dynamic loading via the class loader.
- Python: Enables dynamic modification of objects and classes.

16.3 Exercises

Exercise 1: Comparative Analysis

Choose two OOP languages you are familiar with. Compare and contrast their type systems, encapsulation mechanisms, and support for inheritance.

Exercise 2: Inheritance Experiment

Create a simple class hierarchy in Java or Python. Add at least three classes with inheritance relationships. Implement methods in the superclass and override them in subclasses. Test the behavior of dynamic dispatching.

Solution Example (Java)

```
class Animal {
    public void speak() {
        System.out.println("Animal speaks.");
    }
}

class Dog extends Animal {
    @Override
    public void speak() {
        System.out.println("Dog barks.");
    }
}

```

```
class Cat extends Animal {
    @Override
    public void speak() {
        System.out.println("Cat meows.");
    }
}

public class Main {
    public static void main(String[] args) {
        Animal[] animals =
        { new Dog(), new Cat(), new Animal() };

        for (Animal animal : animals) {
            animal.speak();
        }
    }
}
```

Output:

```
Dog barks.
Cat meows.
Animal speaks.
```

16.4 Summary

OOP languages share fundamental principles but differ in their specific implementations, features, and design philosophies. Understanding these differences is crucial for selecting the right language for a given project and leveraging its strengths effectively.

Chapter 17

Objects, Classes, and Encapsulation

17.1 The Object-Based Core of Java

Java's object-based programming revolves around the concepts of objects and classes. An object is an instance of a class, encapsulating attributes (state) and methods (behavior). Encapsulation ensures that the implementation details of an object are hidden, exposing only the interface for interaction.

17.2 Cloning

Cloning creates a copy of an object. Java provides the `Cloneable` interface for this purpose. By default, cloning in Java is shallow, duplicating only top-level fields. To perform a deep copy, nested objects must be explicitly cloned.

Example: Cloning

```
class Book implements Cloneable {
    String title;

    Book(String title) {
        this.title = title;
    }

    @Override
    protected Object clone()
    throws CloneNotSupportedException {
        return super.clone();
    }
}

public class Main {
    public static void main(String[] args)
    throws CloneNotSupportedException {
        Book original = new Book("Java
        Programming");
        Book copy = (Book) original.clone();
        System.out.println(
        "Original: " + original.title);
```

```
        System.out.println("Copy: " + copy.
        title);
    }
}
```

Output:

```
Original: Java Programming
Copy: Java Programming
```

17.3 Class Methods

Class methods are marked with the `static` keyword. They belong to the class rather than any specific instance and are commonly used for utility functions or operations that do not depend on instance data.

Example: Class Method

```
class Car {
    String color;
    static int numberOfCars;

    Car(String color) {
        this.color = color;
        numberOfCars++;
    }

    static int getTotalCars() {
        return numberOfCars;
```

```
    }
}

public class Main {
    public static void main(String[] args) {
        new Car("Red");
        new Car("Blue");
        System.out.println("
        Total cars: " + Car.getTotalCars());
    }
}
```

Output:

```
Total cars: 2
```

17.4 Class Declarations

Classes define the structure and behavior of objects. A class declaration in Java includes:

- The **name of the class.**
- **Instance variables**: Represent attributes of the object.
- **Methods**: Define the object's behavior.

Example: Class Declaration

```java
class Person {
    String name;
    int age;

    Person(String name, int age) {
        this.name = name;
        this.age = age;
    }

    void displayInfo() {
        System.out.println("
        Name: " + name + ", Age: " + age);
    }
}
```

17.5 Encapsulation and Access Modifiers

Java supports encapsulation through access modifiers:

- **private**: Accessible only within the class.
- **protected**: Accessible within the package and subclasses.
- **public**: Accessible from everywhere.
- **default (no modifier)**: Accessible within the package.

Example: Access Modifiers

```
class BankAccount {
    private double balance;

    BankAccount(double initialBalance) {
        balance = initialBalance;
    }

    public void deposit(double amount) {
        balance += amount;
    }

    public double getBalance() {
        return balance;
    }
}
```

17.6 Exercises

1. Write a program to create a `Product` class with attributes for name, price, and quantity. Add methods to update the price and display product details.

2. Modify the `BankAccount` class to include a method for withdrawal, ensuring that the balance cannot go below zero.

3. Create a class with a static method to calculate the factorial of a number. Test the method with multiple inputs.

Solutions

Solution to Exercise 1:

```
class Product {
    String name;
    double price;
    int quantity;

    Product(String name, double price, int
    quantity) {
        this.name = name;
        this.price = price;
        this.quantity = quantity;
    }

    void updatePrice(double newPrice) {
        price = newPrice;
    }

    void displayDetails() {
        System.out.println("
        Product: " + name + ", Price: " + price
         + ",
        Quantity: " + quantity);
    }
```

```
}
```

Solution to Exercise 2:

```
class BankAccount {
    private double balance;

    BankAccount(double initialBalance) {
        balance = initialBalance;
    }

    public void deposit(double amount) {
        balance += amount;
    }

    public void withdraw(double amount) {
        if (balance >= amount) {
            balance -= amount;
        } else {
            System.out.println("Insufficient
            funds");
        }
    }

    public double getBalance() {
        return balance;
    }
}
```

Solution to Exercise 3:

```
class MathUtil {
    static int factorial(int n) {
        if (n == 0) return 1;
        return n * factorial(n - 1);
    }
}

public class Main {
    public static void main(String[] args) {
        System.out.println("
        Factorial of 5: " + MathUtil.factorial
        (5));
    }
}
```

Output:

```
Factorial of 5: 120
```

Chapter 18

Initialization and Overloading

18.1 Initialization of Variables and Attributes

In object-oriented programming, initialization refers to setting initial values for variables and attributes in a class. Proper initialization ensures that objects begin their lifecycle in a valid state.

18.1.1 Initializing Instance Variables

Instance variables (attributes) are initialized when an object is instantiated. You can initialize them directly or via constructors.

Example:

```java
class Employee {
    String name;
    int age;

    // Constructor initializing variables
    Employee(String name, int age) {
        this.name = name;
        this.age = age;
    }

    void printEmployeeDetails() {
        System.out.println("Employee Name: " +
        name);
        System.out.println("Employee Age: " +
        age);
    }
}

public class Main {
    public static void main(String[] args) {
        Employee emp1 = new Employee("John",
        30);
        emp1.printEmployeeDetails();
        // Outputs: Employee Name: John, Age:
        30
    }
}
```

Explanation: In the above example, the instance

variables **name** and **age** are initialized using the constructor.

18.1.2 Default Initialization

If no constructor is provided, Java provides a default constructor that initializes variables to default values:

- `null` for objects.
- `0` for numbers.
- `false` for booleans.

Example:

```java
class Employee {
    String name;
    int age;

    void printEmployeeDetails() {
        System.out.println("Employee Name: " + name);
        System.out.println("Employee Age: " + age);
    }
}

public class Main {
    public static void main(String[] args) {
        Employee emp1 = new Employee();
        emp1.printEmployeeDetails();
```

```
        // Outputs: Employee Name: null, Age: 0
    }
}
```

18.2 Overloading Methods

18.2.1 What is Method Overloading?

Method overloading allows you to define multiple methods in the same class with the same name but different parameter lists (either by number or type of parameters). It enables methods to perform similar actions on different types of input.

Use Cases for Overloading

- When the same operation needs to be performed on different types of data.
- When you want to provide multiple ways of calling a method.

Example:

```
class Calculator {
    // Method to add two integers
    int add(int a, int b) {
        return a + b;
    }

```

```
    // Overloaded method to add three integers
    int add(int a, int b, int c) {
        return a + b + c;
    }

    // Overloaded method to add two doubles
    double add(double a, double b) {
        return a + b;
    }
}

public class Main {
    public static void main(String[] args) {
        Calculator calc = new Calculator();
        System.out.println(calc.add(2, 3));
        // Outputs 5
        System.out.println(calc.add(2, 3, 4));
        // Outputs 9
        System.out.println(calc.add(2.5, 3.5));
        // Outputs 6.0
    }
}
```

18.2.2 Method Overloading vs. Overriding

- **Method Overloading:** Same method name but different parameters (different types or number of parameters).
- **Method Overriding:** Occurs when a subclass

provides a specific implementation for a method already defined in its superclass.

18.2.3 Best Practices and Common Pitfalls in Overloading

- Ensure the methods with the same name have different parameter types or numbers of parameters.
- Avoid confusion by making sure the overloads are logically distinct in terms of functionality.

Pitfall Example:

```
class Calculator {
    // Incorrect: These methods do the same thing
    int add(int a, int b) {
        return a + b;
    }
    int add(int x, int y) {
        return x + y;
    }
}
```

This could be confusing and error-prone because both methods perform the same task.

Method Overloading vs Method Overriding

- **Method Overloading**:
  - Same method name but different parameters (types or number).
  - Occurs within a single class.
  - Can be done without inheritance.
  - The compiler resolves the method call based on the method signature at compile-time.
  - Used to perform similar operations on different data types or numbers.
- **Method Overriding**:
  - Same method signature (name, parameters, return type) in subclass.
  - Occurs between a superclass and subclass.
  - Requires inheritance (subclass inherits method from superclass).
  - The method call is resolved at runtime using dynamic dispatching.
  - Used to redefine behavior for an inherited method.

Method Overloading Exercise

Problem

Define a class `Calculator` with the following specifications:

- Provide an overloaded `add` method:
  - One version accepts two integers and returns their sum.
  - Another version accepts three integers and returns their sum.
  - A third version accepts two double values and returns their sum.

Tasks

1. Create an instance of `Calculator`.
2. Call each version of the `add` method with appropriate arguments and print the results.

Solution

```
public class Calculator {
    // Method to add two integers
    public int add(int a, int b) {
        return a + b;
    }

```

```
    // Method to add three integers
    public int add(int a, int b, int c) {
        return a + b + c;
    }

    // Method to add two doubles
    public double add(double a, double b) {
        return a + b;
    }

    public static void main(String[] args) {
        Calculator calc = new Calculator();

        System.out.println("Sum of 2 and 3: "
        + calc.add(2, 3));
        System.out.println("Sum of 1, 2, and 3: "
        + calc.add(1, 2, 3));
        System.out.println("Sum of 2.5 and 3.5: "
        + calc.add(2.5, 3.5));
    }
}
```

Expected Output

```
Sum of 2 and 3: 5
Sum of 1, 2, and 3: 6
Sum of 2.5 and 3.5: 6.0
```

18.3 Constructor Overloading

18.3.1 What is Constructor Overloading?

Constructor overloading occurs when a class has multiple constructors with the same name but different parameter lists. This allows objects of the class to be initialized in different ways.

18.3.2 Example of Constructor Overloading

```java
class Employee {
    String name;
    int age;

    // Constructor with one parameter
    Employee(String name) {
        this.name = name;
        this.age = 0; // Default age
    }

    // Constructor with two parameters
    Employee(String name, int age) {
        this.name = name;
        this.age = age;
    }

    void printEmployeeDetails() {
        System.out.println("Employee Name: " +
        name);
```

```java
        System.out.println("Employee Age: " + age);
    }
}

public class Main {
    public static void main(String[] args) {
        Employee emp1 = new Employee("John");
        emp1.printEmployeeDetails();
        // Outputs: Employee Name: John, Age: 0

        Employee emp2 = new Employee("Jane", 30);
        emp2.printEmployeeDetails();
        // Outputs: Employee Name: Jane, Age: 30
    }
}
```

Constructor Overloading Exercise

Problem

Define a class `Book` with the following specifications:

- Include attributes for `title`, `author`, and `price`.
- Provide overloaded constructors:
  - One that accepts only `title`.

  - One that accepts **title** and **author**.
  - One that accepts **title**, **author**, and **price**.

- Add a method `displayDetails` to print the book's details.

Tasks

1. Create instances of `Book` using each of the overloaded constructors.
2. Call `displayDetails` on each instance to verify the outputs.

Solution

```java
public class Book {
    private String title;
    private String author;
    private double price;

    // Constructor with only title
    public Book(String title) {
        this.title = title;
        this.author = "Unknown";
        this.price = 0.0;
    }

    // Constructor with title and author
    public Book(String title, String author) {
```

```java
        this.title = title;
        this.author = author;
        this.price = 0.0;
    }

    // Constructor with title, author, and
    price
    public Book(String title,
    String author,
    double price) {
        this.title = title;
        this.author = author;
        this.price = price;
    }

    // Method to display book details
    public void displayDetails() {
        System.out.println("Title: " + title);
        System.out.println("Author: " + author)
        ;
        System.out.println("Price: $" + price);
    }

    public static void main(String[] args) {
        Book b1 = new Book("1984");
        Book b2 = new Book("To Kill a
        Mockingbird",
        "Harper Lee");
        Book b3 = new Book("The Great Gatsby",
```

```
            "F. Scott Fitzgerald", 10.99);

        b1.displayDetails();
        System.out.println();
        b2.displayDetails();
        System.out.println();
        b3.displayDetails();
    }
}
```

Expected Output

```
Title: 1984
Author: Unknown
Price: $0.0

Title: To Kill a Mockingbird
Author: Harper Lee
Price: $0.0

Title: The Great Gatsby
Author: F. Scott Fitzgerald
Price: $10.99
```

18.4 Conclusion

In this section, we've explored the concepts of variable initialization, method overloading, method overriding, and constructor overloading. We learned how to properly use these features in Java to enhance flexibility and functionality in object-oriented programming.

18.5 Class Methods and Class Attributes

In Java, class methods and class attributes belong to the class itself rather than any specific instance. These are defined using the `static` keyword.

18.5.1 What are Class Methods and Class Attributes?

- **Class Attributes:** Variables declared with the **static** keyword. These are shared across all instances of the class.
- **Class Methods:** Methods declared with the **static** keyword. These can be called without creating an instance of the class.

Example:

```
class Counter {
    static int count = 0; // Class attribute

    // Class method to increment count
    static void increment() {
        count++;
    }
```

```java
}

public class Main {
    public static void main(String[] args) {
    // Accessing class method directly:
        Counter.increment();
        Counter.increment();
        System.out.println("Count: " + Counter.
        count);
        // Outputs: Count: 2
    }
}
```

18.5.2 Use Cases for Class Methods and Attributes

Class methods and attributes are particularly useful in the following scenarios:

1. **Global Constants and Utility Functions:** Static methods can provide utility functions, such as mathematical operations or string manipulations.

```java
    class MathUtil {
        static final double PI = 3.14159;

        static double square(double x) {
            return x * x;
        }
    }
```

```java

    public class Main {
        public static void main(String[]
        args) {
            System.out.println("PI: "
            + MathUtil.PI);
            System.out.println("Square of
            5: "
            + MathUtil.square(5));
            // Outputs: 25.0
        }
    }
```

2. **Controlling Object Creation:** Static methods can enforce specific patterns for object creation, such as the singleton pattern.

```java
    class Singleton {
        private static Singleton instance;

        private Singleton() {
            // Private constructor
        }

        static Singleton getInstance() {
            if (instance == null) {
                instance = new Singleton();
            }
            return instance;
        }
```

```
}

public class Main {
    public static void main(String[]
    args) {
        Singleton obj =
        Singleton.getInstance();
    }
}
```

3. **Subclass-Specific Object Creation:** Factory methods can determine which subclass instance to create based on certain conditions.

```
abstract class Shape {
    abstract void draw();
}

class Circle extends Shape {
    void draw() {
        System.out.println("Drawing a
        circle");
    }
}

class Rectangle extends Shape {
    void draw() {
        System.out.println("
        Drawing a rectangle");
    }
```

```
}

class ShapeFactory {
    static Shape getShape(String type) {
    if (type.equalsIgnoreCase("circle")) {
            return new Circle();
        } else
    if (type.equalsIgnoreCase("rectangle")) {
            return new Rectangle();
        }
        return null;
    }
}

public class Main {
    public static void main(String[] args) {
        Shape shape =
        ShapeFactory.getShape("circle");
        shape.draw();
        // Outputs: Drawing a circle
    }
}
```

4. **Tracking Instance Information:** Static at-

tributes can track information across all instances, such as a counter for the number of objects created.

```java
class Employee {
// Tracks total employees:
    static int employeeCount = 0;
    String name;

    Employee(String name) {
        this.name = name;
        employeeCount++;
    }
}

public class Main {
    public static void main(String[]
    args) {
        Employee e1 = new Employee("
        John");
        Employee e2 = new Employee("
        Jane");
        System.out.println("Total
        Employees: "
        + Employee.employeeCount);
        // Outputs: 2
    }
}
```

18.5.3 When to Use Class Methods and Attributes

- Use class methods for operations that do not depend on instance-specific data.
- Use class attributes when a property or value is shared across all instances of the class.

18.5.4 Best Practices and Common Pitfalls

- Avoid overusing static attributes, as they can make testing and debugging difficult.
- Clearly distinguish between operations meant for individual objects and those meant for the class as a whole.
- Be cautious about thread safety when modifying static attributes in multi-threaded applications.

18.6 Conlusion

Class methods and attributes are shared across all instances of a class, making them ideal for global constants, modular functionality, and managing shared resources. Used wisely, they enhance efficiency and clarity, but overuse can reduce flexibility and introduce dependencies. Balance is key.

Chapter 19

Recursive Class Declarations in Java

19.1 Introduction to Recursive Class Declarations

Recursive class declarations involve classes that reference themselves, either directly or indirectly. This approach is fundamental for implementing dynamic and flexible data structures like lists, trees, and graphs, which are widely used in programming.

For instance, a `Node` class in a linked list often contains a reference to the next node, demonstrating recursion.

19.2 Overview of Containers

Containers are classes designed to hold and manage multiple elements. They simplify data management by providing functionalities like adding, removing, and iterating over elements. In Java, the `java.util` package provides a variety of container classes, such as `ArrayList` and `LinkedList`. These containers make it easier to store and manipulate groups of objects.

19.3 The `java.util` Package

The `java.util` package offers essential data structures and utility classes for Java programs. Some of the key classes include:

- `ArrayList`: Provides dynamic array functionality.
- `LinkedList`: Implements doubly-linked lists.
- `HashSet` and `HashMap`: Support unique elements and fast lookups.

19.4 Lists in Java

Lists are ordered collections of elements. In Java, lists are part of the `java.util` package. The most common implementations are `ArrayList` and `LinkedList`. Each implementation has distinct advantages:

- **ArrayList**: Suitable for random access and resizing arrays. It allows for fast access to elements by index, but adding or removing elements in the middle can be inefficient.

- **LinkedList**: Optimal for frequent insertions and deletions. It is slower for random access but excels at adding or removing elements from the beginning or end of the list.

19.4.1 Example: Using a List in Java

```java
import java.util.ArrayList;

public class ListExample {
    public static void main(String[] args) {
        ArrayList<String> tasks = new ArrayList
            <>();
        tasks.add("Study recursion");
        tasks.add("Write Java code");
        tasks.add("Test the program");

        System.out.println("Tasks to do:");
        for (String task : tasks) {
            System.out.println(task);
        }
    }
}
/*
Output:
```

```
Tasks to do:
Study recursion
Write Java code
Test the program
*/
```

19.5 Understanding LinkedList

A LinkedList is implemented using nodes, where each node contains data and references to the next (and sometimes the previous) node. This structure makes insertion and deletion efficient, especially when managing large amounts of data with frequent changes.

19.5.1 Example: LinkedList Implementation

```
import java.util.LinkedList;

public class LinkedListExample {
    public static void main(String[] args) {
        LinkedList<String> queue = new
        LinkedList<>();
        queue.add("First");
        queue.add("Second");
        queue.add("Third");

        System.out.println("Queue: " + queue);
        System.out.println("Polling: " +
```

```
            queue.poll());
            // Removes the first element
            System.out.println("
            Queue after polling: " + queue);
    }
}
/*
Output:
Queue: [First, Second, Third]
Polling: First
Queue after polling: [Second, Third]
*/
```

19.6 Recursive Class for Entry Objects

A linked list can be implemented using `Entry` objects that store data and a reference to the next object. This demonstrates recursion in the design of the data structure.

19.6.1 Example: Recursive Entry Class

```
class Entry {
    String data;
    Entry next;

    Entry(String data) {
        this.data = data;
```

```
        this.next = null;
    }
}

public class EntryExample {
    public static void main(String[] args) {
        Entry head = new Entry("Node1");
        head.next = new Entry("Node2");
        head.next.next = new Entry("Node3");

        Entry current = head;
        while (current != null) {
            System.out.print(current.data + "
            -> ");
            current = current.next;
        }
        System.out.println("null");
    }
}
/*
Output:
Node1 -> Node2 -> Node3 -> null
*/
```

19.7 Exercises

Exercise 1: Implement a Custom Linked List

Write a class `MyLinkedList` with the following methods:

- Add elements to the head or tail of the list.
- Remove an element by its value.
- Print all elements in the list.

Solution:

```
class MyLinkedList {
    private static class Node {
        String data;
        Node next;

        Node(String data) {
            this.data = data;
        }
    }

    private Node head;

    public void addToHead(String data) {
        Node newNode = new Node(data);
        newNode.next = head;
        head = newNode;
    }

    public void addToTail(String data) {
        if (head == null) {
            head = new Node(data);
            return;
        }
```

```
        Node current = head;
        while (current.next != null) {
            current = current.next;
        }
        current.next = new Node(data);
    }

    public void remove(String data) {
        if (head == null) return;
        if (head.data.equals(data)) {
            head = head.next;
            return;
        }
        Node current = head;
        while (current.next != null &&
        !current.next.data.equals(data)) {
            current = current.next;
        }
        if (current.next != null) {
            current.next = current.next.next;
        }
    }

    public void printAll() {
        Node current = head;
        while (current != null) {
            System.out.print(current.data + "
            -> ");
            current = current.next;
```

```
        }
        System.out.println("null");
    }
}

public class MyLinkedListExample {
    public static void main(String[] args) {
        MyLinkedList list = new MyLinkedList();
        list.addToHead("Node1");
        list.addToTail("Node2");
        list.addToTail("Node3");
        list.printAll();

        list.remove("Node2");
        list.printAll();
    }
}
/*
Output:
Node1 -> Node2 -> Node3 -> null
Node1 -> Node3 -> null
*/
```

Exercise 2: Implement a Custom ArrayList

Now, implement a custom version of the `ArrayList` class with basic functionalities such as adding an element, removing an element, and printing all elements.

Solution:

```
class MyArrayList {
    private String[] array;
    private int size;

    public MyArrayList() {
        array = new String[10]; // initial capacity
        size = 0;
    }

    public void add(String data) {
        if (size == array.length) {
            // Resize the array if needed
            String[] newArray =
            new String[array.length * 2];
            System.arraycopy(
            array, 0, newArray, 0, array.length);
            array = newArray;
        }
        array[size++] = data;
    }

    public void remove(String data) {
        for (int i = 0; i < size; i++) {
            if (array[i].equals(data)) {
        // Shift elements left to remove the element
                for (int j = i; j < size - 1; j
```

```
                ++) {
                    array[j] = array[j + 1];
                }
                array[--size] = null;
        // Decrease size and nullify the last
        element
                return;
            }
        }
    }

    public void printAll() {
        for (int i = 0; i < size; i++) {
            System.out.print(array[i] + " ");
        }
        System.out.println();
    }
}

public class MyArrayListExample {
    public static void main(String[] args) {
        MyArrayList list = new MyArrayList();
        list.add("Element1");
        list.add("Element2");
        list.add("Element3");
        list.printAll();
        // Expected: Element1 Element2 Element3

        list.remove("Element2");
```

```
        list.printAll();
        // Expected: Element1 Element3
    }
}
/*
Output:
Element1 Element2 Element3
Element1 Element3
*/
```

19.8 Summary

This chapter explored recursive class declarations and their applications in Java. Key points include:

- Recursive classes enable the implementation of data structures like linked lists and trees.
- Containers in the `java.util` package provide essential utilities for data management.
- `LinkedList` and recursive `Entry` classes showcase the power of recursion in data structure design.
- `ArrayList` and `LinkedList` offer distinct advantages depending on use cases, with `ArrayList` excelling in random access and `LinkedList` being more efficient for insertions and deletions.

Through examples and exercises, readers should now be familiar with designing, implementing, and testing recursive data structures in Java.

Chapter 20

Encapsulation in Java

20.1 Introduction to Encapsulation

Encapsulation is one of the four fundamental principles of object-oriented programming, alongside inheritance, polymorphism, and abstraction. It focuses on restricting access to certain parts of an object's data and functionality, ensuring that internal implementation details remain hidden from the outside world.

This chapter will explore how encapsulation promotes robust, maintainable, and secure code.

20.2 Why Encapsulation?

Encapsulation ensures that:

1. **Consistency Criteria:** Users of a class cannot

violate its rules or misuse its objects, maintaining the class's integrity.

2. **Implementation Independence:** Implementation details can change without affecting the rest of the system, provided the interface remains stable. This allows flexibility and reduces dependency.

3. **Information Hiding:** Encapsulation hides internal data and implementation logic, protecting it from unwanted access or modification.

20.3 Mechanisms of Encapsulation

20.3.1 Access Modifiers

Java provides four access levels to control the visibility of classes, methods, and attributes:

- `private`: Accessible only within the same class.
- `default` (no modifier): Accessible within the same package.
- `protected`: Accessible within the same package and subclasses.
- `public`: Accessible from anywhere.

20.3.2 Separating Interfaces

Encapsulation involves separating the **public interface** (methods intended for use by external code) from the **private implementation** (internal workings of the class).

20.3.3 Class Invariants

A class invariant is a condition that holds true for the state of an object throughout its lifetime. Proper encapsulation ensures invariants are respected.

20.3.4 Read-Only Methods vs. State-Modifying Methods

- **Read-Only Methods:** Provide access to object data without altering it, e.g., `getFirstName()`.
- **State-Modifying Methods:** Change the internal state of an object, e.g., `setFirstName()`.

20.4 Example: Implementing Encapsulation

20.4.1 Encapsulation in a `Person` Class

```java
public class Person {
    private String firstName;
    private String lastName;
```

```

    // Constructor
    public Person(String firstName, String lastName) {
        this.firstName = firstName;
        this.lastName = lastName;
    }

    // Getter for firstName (read-only)
    public String getFirstName() {
        return firstName;
    }

    // Setter for firstName (state-modifying)
    public void setFirstName(String firstName) {
        if (firstName != null &&
        !firstName.isEmpty()) {
            this.firstName = firstName;
        } else {
            System.out.println("Invalid name!");
        }
    }

    // Getter for lastName
    public String getLastName() {
        return lastName;
    }
```

```java

    // Setter for lastName
    public void setLastName(String lastName) {
        if (lastName != null && !lastName.
        isEmpty()) {
            this.lastName = lastName;
        } else {
            System.out.println("Invalid name!");

        }
    }
}
```

20.4.2 Main Method: Testing the Person Class

```java
public class Main {
    public static void main(String[] args) {
        Person person = new Person("John", "Doe
        ");
        System.out.println("First Name: " +
        person.getFirstName());
        System.out.println("Last Name: " +
        person.getLastName());

        person.setFirstName("Jane");
        System.out.println("Updated First Name:
         " +
        person.getFirstName());
```

```

        person.setLastName("");
        System.out.println("Updated Last Name:
        " +
        person.getLastName());
    }
}
```

Output:

```
First Name: John
Last Name: Doe
Updated First Name: Jane
Invalid name!
Updated Last Name: Doe
```

20.5 Exercises

Exercise 1: Encapsulation in a Bank Account

Write a `BankAccount` class with the following:

- `private double balance`
- `public void deposit(double amount)`
- `public void withdraw(double amount)`
- Ensure withdrawals cannot result in a negative balance.

Solution:

```
public class BankAccount {
    private double balance;

    public BankAccount(double initialBalance) {

        if (initialBalance >= 0) {
            this.balance = initialBalance;
        } else {
            System.out.println("
            Initial balance must be non-
            negative.");
            this.balance = 0;
        }
    }

    public double getBalance() {
        return balance;
    }

    public void deposit(double amount) {
        if (amount > 0) {
            balance += amount;
        } else {
            System.out.println("
            Deposit amount must be positive.");
        }
    }
```

```java

    public void withdraw(double amount) {
        if (amount > 0 && balance >= amount) {
            balance -= amount;
        } else {
            System.out.println("
            Invalid withdrawal amount or
            insufficient balance.");
        }
    }
}
```

Main Method:

```java
public class BankAccountTest {
    public static void main(String[] args) {
        BankAccount account = new BankAccount
        (100.0);
        System.out.println("Initial Balance: $"
         +
        account.getBalance());

        account.deposit(50.0);
        System.out.println("After Deposit: $" +
        account.getBalance());

        account.withdraw(30.0);
        System.out.println("After Withdrawal: $
        " +
```

```
        account.getBalance());

        account.withdraw(150.0);
    }
}
```

Output:

```
Initial Balance: $100.0
After Deposit: $150.0
After Withdrawal: $120.0
Invalid withdrawal amount or insufficient balance.
```

Exercise 2: Validating Input in Encapsulation

Modify the `Person` class to include age with the following conditions:

- The age must be a positive integer.
- Add `getAge()` and `setAge(int age)` methods.

Solution:

```
public class Person {
    private String firstName;
    private String lastName;
    private int age;

    public Person(String firstName,
    String lastName,
```

```
    int age) {
        this.firstName = firstName;
        this.lastName = lastName;
        setAge(age);
    }

    public int getAge() {
        return age;
    }

    public void setAge(int age) {
        if (age > 0) {
            this.age = age;
        } else {
            System.out.println("
            Age must be positive.");
        }
    }
}
```

Main Method:

```
public class PersonTest {
    public static void main(String[] args) {
        Person person =
        new Person("Alice", "Smith", 25);
        System.out.println("Age: " +
        person.getAge());

```

```
        person.setAge(30);
        System.out.println("Updated Age: " +
        person.getAge());

        person.setAge(-5);
    }
}
```

Output:

```
Age: 25
Updated Age: 30
Age must be positive.
```

20.6 Summary

Encapsulation is a cornerstone of object-oriented programming, fostering:

- **Code Reusability:** By separating interfaces from implementations.
- **Safety:** By preventing unauthorized or unintended access.
- **Flexibility:** By allowing internal implementation changes without disrupting external code.

Through examples and exercises, you have learned how encapsulation safeguards the integrity of objects, simplifies maintenance, and encourages better software design practices.

Chapter 21

Structuring Classes in Java

21.1 Introduction to Class Structuring

Class structuring in Java allows developers to design clean, modular, and encapsulated systems. Inner classes play a key role in organizing related functionality and ensuring a tight coupling between outer and inner classes when needed.

Java supports several types of inner classes:

- **Non-static inner classes**: Depend on an instance of the outer class.
- **Static inner classes**: Independent of outer class instances.

21.2 Inner Classes

Inner classes are defined within an outer class, providing a way to logically group classes that are only used in one place. They have access to the outer class's members (even private ones).

Example: Basic Inner Class Usage

```java
class OuterClass {
    private String message = "Hello from Outer Class";

    class InnerClass {
        void displayMessage() {
            System.out.println(message);
        }
    }

    public void showInner() {
        InnerClass inner = new InnerClass();
        inner.displayMessage();
    }
}

public class InnerClassExample {
    public static void main(String[] args) {
        OuterClass outer = new OuterClass();
        outer.showInner();
```

```
    }
}
```

Expected Output:

```
Hello from Outer Class
```

Explanation:

- The **InnerClass** has access to the private member **message** of **OuterClass**.
- The outer class controls the instantiation and usage of the inner class through the `showInner` method.

21.3 Static Inner Classes

Static inner classes are nested classes marked with the **static** keyword. They do not require an instance of the outer class and can access static members of the outer class.

Example: Static Inner Class Usage

```
class OuterClass {
    static String staticMessage =
    "Hello from Static Inner Class";

    static class StaticInnerClass {
        void displayMessage() {
            System.out.println(staticMessage);
```

```java
        }
    }
}

public class StaticInnerClassExample {
    public static void main(String[] args) {
        OuterClass.StaticInnerClass inner =
        new OuterClass.StaticInnerClass();
        inner.displayMessage();
    }
}
```

Expected Output:

```
Hello from Static Inner Class
```

Explanation:

- `StaticInnerClass` can access the `staticMessage` field of `OuterClass` without needing an instance of `OuterClass`.
- The `StaticInnerClass` is instantiated directly using the outer class name.

21.4 Non-Static Inner Classes

Non-static inner classes are tied to an instance of the outer class. They can access all members of the outer class, including instance variables and methods.

Example: Non-Static Inner Class Usage

```java
class OuterClass {
    private String instanceMessage =
    "Hello from Non-Static Inner Class";

    class NonStaticInnerClass {
        void displayMessage() {
            System.out.println(instanceMessage);

        }
    }
}

public class NonStaticInnerClassExample {
    public static void main(String[] args) {
        OuterClass outer = new OuterClass();
        OuterClass.NonStaticInnerClass inner =
        outer.new NonStaticInnerClass();
        inner.displayMessage();
    }
}
```

Expected Output:

```
Hello from Non-Static Inner Class
```

Explanation:

- `NonStaticInnerClass` requires an instance of `OuterClass` to be created.

- The syntax **outer.new NonStaticInnerClass()** creates the inner class tied to the `outer` instance.

21.5 Advantages and Use Cases

- **Static Inner Classes**:
  - Suitable for utility classes (e.g., `MathHelper`).
  - Saves memory as they don't hold a reference to the outer class.
  - Good for modularity.
- **Non-Static Inner Classes**:
  - Useful for classes that need access to outer class members.
  - Ideal for implementing functionality that is tightly coupled with the outer class.

21.6 Exercises

Exercise 1: Creating an Inner Class

Write an outer class `Library` with an inner class `Book`. `Book` should have attributes like `title` and `author` and a method to display its details. The outer class should have a method to create and display a list of books.

Solution:

```
class Library {
    class Book {
        String title;
        String author;

        Book(String title, String author) {
            this.title = title;
            this.author = author;
        }

        void displayBookInfo() {
            System.out.println("Title: " +
            title + ", Author: " + author);
        }
    }

    public void showLibrary() {
        Book book1 = new Book("1984",
        "George Orwell");
        Book book2 = new Book("To Kill a
        Mockingbird",
        "Harper Lee");

        book1.displayBookInfo();
        book2.displayBookInfo();
    }
}
```

```java

public class LibraryExample {
    public static void main(String[] args) {
        Library library = new Library();
        library.showLibrary();
    }
}
```

Expected Output:

```
Title: 1984, Author: George Orwell
Title: To Kill a Mockingbird, Author: Harper Lee
```

Exercise 2: Using Static Inner Classes

Implement a **MathHelper** class with a static inner class **FactorialCalculator** that calculates the factorial of a number.

Solution:

```java
class MathHelper {
    static class FactorialCalculator {
        int calculateFactorial(int n) {
            int result = 1;
            for (int i = 1; i <= n; i++) {
                result *= i;
            }
            return result;
        }
```

```
    }
}

public class MathHelperExample {
    public static void main(String[] args) {
        MathHelper.FactorialCalculator
        calculator =
        new MathHelper.FactorialCalculator();
        int factorialOf5 =
        calculator.calculateFactorial(5);
        System.out.println("
        Factorial of 5: " + factorialOf5);
    }
}
```

Expected Output:

```
Factorial of 5: 120
```

21.7 Summary

- **Inner classes** encapsulate functionality tightly bound to the outer class.
- **Static inner classes** are suitable for utility-like structures, saving memory and enhancing modularity.
- **Non-static inner classes** enable direct access to instance variables and methods of the outer class.

By mastering inner classes, developers can achieve better class organization and encapsulation in Java programs.

Chapter 22

Structuring Programs with Packages in Java

22.1 Introduction to Packages

Packages in Java serve as a mechanism to organize and modularize code. They allow developers to group related classes and interfaces, manage namespaces, control access rights, and prevent naming conflicts. Packages also help maintain a clean project structure by organizing code into a hierarchical tree.

A package declaration appears at the top of a Java file, followed by import statements and type declarations. The syntax is as follows:

```
package package_name;
import other_packages.*;
```

```
public class ClassName {
    // Class body
}
```

22.2 The Purpose of Packages

The primary objectives of using packages include:

- Organizing and maintaining related classes and interfaces.
- Controlling access rights and ensuring encapsulation.
- Preventing name conflicts in large projects.
- Structuring projects hierarchically using the file system.

22.3 Creating and Using Packages

Packages can be created by declaring them at the top of a Java file and placing the file in the corresponding directory. This allows classes from the package to be used elsewhere using import statements.

22.3.1 Example: Creating and Using Packages

```java
// File: library/Book.java
package library;

public class Book {
    private String title;

    public Book(String title) {
        this.title = title;
    }

    public String getTitle() {
        return title;
    }
}

// File: library/User.java
package library;

public class User {
    private String name;

    public User(String name) {
        this.name = name;
    }

    public String getName() {
        return name;
    }
}
```

```

// File: Main.java
import library.Book;
import library.User;

public class Main {
    public static void main(String[] args) {
        Book book = new Book("Java Programming"
        );
        User user = new User("Alice");
        System.out.println(user.getName() +
        " borrowed " + book.getTitle());
    }
}
```

Expected Output:

```
Alice borrowed Java Programming
```

Exercise 1: Create Your Own Package

Write a program to define a package named **shapes** containing classes `Circle` and `Rectangle`. Each class should have methods to calculate the area. Use these classes in a `Main` program.

Solution:

```
// File: shapes/Circle.java
package shapes;

public class Circle {
```

```
    private double radius;

    public Circle(double radius) {
        this.radius = radius;
    }

    public double calculateArea() {
        return Math.PI * radius * radius;
    }
}

// File: shapes/Rectangle.java
package shapes;

public class Rectangle {
    private double length, width;

    public Rectangle(double length, double
    width) {
        this.length = length;
        this.width = width;
    }

    public double calculateArea() {
        return length * width;
    }
}

// File: Main.java
```

```java
import shapes.Circle;
import shapes.Rectangle;

public class Main {
    public static void main(String[] args) {
        Circle circle = new Circle(5);
        Rectangle rectangle = new Rectangle(4, 6);

        System.out.println("Circle Area: " +
        circle.calculateArea());
        System.out.println("Rectangle Area: " +
        rectangle.calculateArea());
    }
}
```

Expected Output:

```
Circle Area: 78.53981633974483
Rectangle Area: 24.0
```

22.4 Encapsulation at the Package Level

Packages provide a way to encapsulate classes and interfaces. The access modifiers `public`, `protected`, and default (package-private) determine accessibility at the package level.

22.4.1 Example: Controlling Access with Packages

```
// File: library/Author.java
package library;

class Author { // Default access
    private String name;

    Author(String name) {
        this.name = name;
    }

    String getName() {
        return name;
    }
}

// File: library/Book.java
package library;

public class Book {
    private String title;
    private Author author;

    public Book(String title, String
    authorName) {
        this.title = title;
        this.author = new Author(authorName);
```

```
    }

    public String getDetails() {
        return title + " by " + author.getName
        ();
    }
}

// File: Main.java
import library.Book;

public class Main {
    public static void main(String[] args) {
        Book book =
        new Book("Effective Java", "Joshua
        Bloch");
        System.out.println(book.getDetails());
    }
}
```

Expected Output:

```
Effective Java by Joshua Bloch
```

Exercise 2: Experiment with Access Levels

Modify the `Author` class to use `public` access instead of default access. Observe how this changes the ability to instantiate `Author` objects outside the `library` package.

Solution: Making `Author` public allows external

access and instantiation. Encapsulation is compromised if internal classes are made public unnecessarily.

22.5 Handling Name Conflicts

Name conflicts can occur when multiple packages define classes with the same name. Fully qualified names or import statements help resolve these conflicts.

22.5.1 Example: Resolving Name Conflicts

```java
// File: library/science/Book.java
package library.science;

public class Book {
    public String getTitle() {
        return "Science Book";
    }
}

// File: library/literature/Book.java
package library.literature;

public class Book {
    public String getTitle() {
        return "Literature Book";
    }
}

```

```
// File: Main.java
import library.science.Book as ScienceBook;
import library.literature.Book as
LiteratureBook;

public class Main {
    public static void main(String[] args) {
        ScienceBook scienceBook = new
        ScienceBook();
        LiteratureBook literatureBook =
        new LiteratureBook();
        System.out.println(scienceBook.getTitle
        ());
        System.out.println(literatureBook.
        getTitle());
    }
}
```

Expected Output:

```
Science Book
Literature Book
```

Exercise 3: Use Fully Qualified Names

Rewrite the example above without using `import` statements. Use fully qualified names instead.

Solution

Using fully qualified names eliminates the need for import aliases but can make code harder to read. This approach is demonstrated in the code below.

```
public class Main {
    public static void main(String[] args) {
        library.science.Book scienceBook =
        new library.science.Book();
        library.literature.Book literatureBook =
        new library.literature.Book();

        System.out.println("Science Book: " +
        scienceBook.getTitle());
        System.out.println("Literature Book: " +
        literatureBook.getTitle());
    }
}
```

Explanation

In this solution:

Fully qualified names like **library.science.Book** and **library.literature.Book** are used whenever a class from a specific package is referenced. This approach avoids the use of **import** statements or aliases, resolving naming conflicts directly. While functional, this approach may reduce code readability in larger programs.

Expected Output

```
Science Book: Science Book
Literature Book: Literature Book
```

Using fully qualified names eliminates the need for import aliases but can make code harder to read. This approach is demonstrated in the code.

22.6 Summary

This chapter explored Java packages as a way to structure programs, ensure encapsulation, manage namespaces, and resolve naming conflicts. Through examples and exercises, you learned how to create, use, and manage packages effectively. This understanding is fundamental for organizing and maintaining complex Java programs.

Chapter 23

Class Relations in Object-Oriented Design

23.1 Object-Oriented Design Overview

Object-oriented design (OOD) focuses on structuring programs around objects and their interactions. It seeks to identify and classify the key abstractions of a task area while eliminating unnecessary details. This process includes:

1. Identifying objects of a task area, classifying them, and refining them to essential abstractions (key abstractions).

2. Designing relationships between objects to create an intuitive and dynamic model.

23.2 Uses-Relation

An object X uses another object Y when:

- A method of X sends a message to Y.
- A method of X creates Y.
- Y is passed as a parameter to X.
- A method of X returns Y as a result.

Example: Uses-Relation

The following example illustrates the uses-relation:

```
class Author {
    private String name;

    public Author(String name) {
        this.name = name;
    }

    public String getName() {
        return name;
    }
}

```

```java
class Book {
    private Author author;

    public Book(String authorName) {
        this.author = new Author(authorName);
    }

    public void printAuthor() {
        System.out.println("Author: " +
        author.getName());
    }
}

public class Main {
    public static void main(String[] args) {
        Book book = new Book("Jane Austen");
        book.printAuthor();
    }
}
```

Expected Output:

```
Author: Jane Austen
```

Exercise 1: Uses-Relation

Modify the example so that the book object can return the name of its author directly through a method `getAuthorName()`.

Solution:

```
class Author {
    private String name;

    public Author(String name) {
        this.name = name;
    }

    public String getName() {
        return name;
    }
}

class Book {
    private Author author;

    public Book(String authorName) {
        this.author = new Author(authorName);
    }

    public String getAuthorName() {
        return author.getName();
    }
}

public class Main {
    public static void main(String[] args) {
        Book book = new Book("Jane Austen");
        System.out.println("Author Name: " +
        book.getAuthorName());
```

```
    }
}
```

Expected Output:

```
Author Name: Jane Austen
```

23.3 Accessibility-Relation

An object X can access another object Y if Y is reachable through repeated attribute selections starting from X. This accessibility impacts which objects can be affected by changes or method calls.

Example: Accessibility-Relation

The following example demonstrates accessibility:

```
class Engine {
    private String type;

    public Engine(String type) {
        this.type = type;
    }

    public String getType() {
        return type;
    }
}

class Car {
```

```
    private Engine engine;

    public Car(String engineType) {
        this.engine = new Engine(engineType);
    }

    public String getEngineType() {
        return engine.getType();
    }
}

public class Main {
    public static void main(String[] args) {
        Car car = new Car("V8");
        System.out.println("Engine Type: " +
        car.getEngineType());
    }
}
```

Expected Output:

```
Engine Type: V8
```

Exercise 2: Accessibility-Relation

Extend the example so that the car object can set a new engine type.

Solution:

```
class Engine {
    private String type;
```

```java

    public Engine(String type) {
        this.type = type;
    }

    public String getType() {
        return type;
    }

    public void setType(String type) {
        this.type = type;
    }
}

class Car {
    private Engine engine;

    public Car(String engineType) {
        this.engine = new Engine(engineType);
    }

    public String getEngineType() {
        return engine.getType();
    }

    public void setEngineType(String newType) {
        engine.setType(newType);
    }
```

```
}

public class Main {
    public static void main(String[] args) {
        Car car = new Car("V8");
        System.out.println("Initial Engine Type
        : " +
        car.getEngineType());
        car.setEngineType("Electric");
        System.out.println("Updated Engine Type
        : " +
        car.getEngineType());
    }
}
```

Expected Output:

```
Initial Engine Type: V8
Updated Engine Type: Electric
```

23.4 Is-A Relation

The *is-a* relation describes the relationship between objects and their types. For example, if B is a subtype of A, then every object of type B is also of type A.

Example: Is-A Relation

The following example demonstrates the is-a relation using inheritance:

```java
class Animal {
    public void makeSound() {
        System.out.println("Some generic sound ...");
    }
}

class Dog extends Animal {
    @Override
    public void makeSound() {
        System.out.println("Bark");
    }
}

public class Main {
    public static void main(String[] args) {
        Animal myDog = new Dog();
        myDog.makeSound();
    }
}
```

Expected Output:

```
Bark
```

Exercise 3: Is-A Relation

Add another subclass, `Cat`, which overrides the `makeSound` method, and update the main program to demonstrate polymorphism.

Solution:

```
class Animal {
    public void makeSound() {
        System.out.println("Some generic sound
        ...");
    }
}

class Dog extends Animal {
    @Override
    public void makeSound() {
        System.out.println("Bark");
    }
}

class Cat extends Animal {
    @Override
    public void makeSound() {
        System.out.println("Meow");
    }
}

public class Main {
    public static void main(String[] args) {
        Animal myDog = new Dog();
        Animal myCat = new Cat();
        myDog.makeSound();
        myCat.makeSound();
    }
```

```
}
```

Expected Output:

```
Bark
Meow
```

Chapter 24

The Aims of Type Systems

Introduction

Type systems play a fundamental role in programming languages by enforcing rules about how data can be used and combined. These rules help prevent errors, promote clarity, and facilitate maintainable code. In this chapter, we explore the aims of type systems, discuss their advantages and limitations, and examine remedies for their shortcomings.

24.1 What Are Type Declarations?

Overview: Type declarations define the kinds of values variables can hold. They help the compiler enforce rules about how these variables are used, catching many errors before runtime.

Example:

```
int age = 25;
String name = "Alice";
```

Here, `age` is declared as an integer, and `name` as a string.

Exercise 1: Declare variables for:

- A double to hold the price of an item.
- A boolean to check if the item is in stock.

Solution:

```
double price = 49.99;
boolean isInStock = true;
```

No output, but the variables are declared with type safety.

24.2 Static vs. Dynamic Types

Overview:

- **Static Typing:** Variables' types are fixed at compile time (e.g., Java, C++).

- **Dynamic Typing:** Variables' types are determined at runtime (e.g., Python, JavaScript).

Example:

```
int number = 10; // Static typing
```

In Python:

```
number = 10 # Dynamic typing
number = "Ten" # Allowed in dynamic typing
```

Exercise 2: Explain the benefits of static typing over dynamic typing.

Solution: Static typing detects type errors at compile time, improving safety and performance. For example:

```
int x = "String"; // Error caught at compile
time
```

24.3 Static Type Safety

Overview: Static type safety ensures that operations involving incompatible types are prevented during compilation, reducing runtime errors.

Example:

```
int x = 10;
String y = "Hello";
// System.out.println(x + y); // Compile-time
error
```

Exercise 3: Create a program where you attempt an invalid operation between incompatible types. Observe the error.

Solution:

```
int num = 5;
String text = "Text";
// int result = num + text;
// Compile-time error: incompatible types
```

Explanation: Java prevents adding an integer to a string directly without explicit type conversion.

24.4 Disadvantages of Type Systems

Overview: While type systems provide safety and clarity, they can also introduce challenges:

- **Inflexibility:** Restricting operations between types.
- **Larger Code:** Requiring explicit type declarations.

24.5 Remedies: Subtyping

Overview: Subtyping allows a type to inherit properties from another type, enabling flexibility in handling objects.

Example:

```java
class Animal {}
class Dog extends Animal {}

Animal pet = new Dog(); // Subtyping
```

Subtyping lets **pet** refer to any subclass of **Animal**.

Exercise 4: Write a program that uses subtyping to create a flexible animal shelter system.

Solution:

```java
class Animal {
    public void sound() {
        System.out.println("Some sound...");
    }
}

class Dog extends Animal {
    public void sound() {
        System.out.println("Woof!");
    }
}

class Cat extends Animal {
    public void sound() {
        System.out.println("Meow!");
    }
}

public class Shelter {
    public static void main(String[] args) {
```

```java
        Animal myPet = new Dog();
        myPet.sound(); // Output: Woof!

        myPet = new Cat();
        myPet.sound(); // Output: Meow!
    }
}
```

Explanation: Subtyping allows `myPet` to switch between different animal types.

24.6 Remedies: Parameterization

Overview: Parameterization, such as generics in Java, makes code more reusable and type-safe.

Example:

```java
import java.util.ArrayList;

ArrayList<String> names = new ArrayList<>();
names.add("Alice");
```

Exercise 5: Create a generic class to store items of any type.

Solution:

```java
class Box<T> {
    private T item;

    public void setItem(T item) {
        this.item = item;
```

```
    }

    public T getItem() {
        return item;
    }
}

public class Main {
    public static void main(String[] args) {
        Box<String> stringBox = new Box<>();
        stringBox.setItem("Hello");
        System.out.println(stringBox.getItem())
        ;
        // Output: Hello

        Box<Integer> intBox = new Box<>();
        intBox.setItem(42);
        System.out.println(intBox.getItem());
        // Output: 42
    }
}
```

24.7 java.lang.Object

Overview: In Java, `java.lang.Object` is the root class, allowing objects of any type to be handled generically.

Example:

```
Object obj = "Hello";
```

```
System.out.println(obj.toString());
// Output: Hello
```

Exercise 6: Write a method that accepts `Object` and prints its class type.

Solution:

```
public class Main {
    public static void printType(Object obj) {
        System.out.println("Type: " +
        obj.getClass().getName());
    }

    public static void main(String[] args) {
        printType("String");
        printType(123);
        printType(45.67);
    }
}
// Output:
// Type: java.lang.String
// Type: java.lang.Integer
// Type: java.lang.Double
```

24.8 Type Casting

Overview: Type casting allows converting an object from one type to another, with care to avoid runtime errors.

Example:

```
Object obj = "Hello";
String str = (String) obj;
System.out.println(str); // Output: Hello
```

Exercise 7: Demonstrate safe and unsafe casting with an example.

Solution:

```
public class Main {
    public static void main(String[] args) {
        Object obj = "Hello";

        // Safe casting
        // instanceof checks if obj is of type
        String:
        if (obj instanceof String) {
            String str = (String) obj;
            System.out.println("Safe Casting: "
             + str);
            // Output: Hello
        }

        // Unsafe casting
        try {
        // Causes ClassCastException:
            Integer num = (Integer) obj;
        } catch (ClassCastException e) {
            System.out.println("Unsafe Casting:
             " +
```

```
                e.getMessage());
            }
        }
    }
```

Explanation: Using `instanceof` ensures safe casting, avoiding runtime exceptions.

Conclusion

Type systems provide safety and structure in programming but require careful handling to balance flexibility and safety. Techniques like subtyping, parameterization, and type casting enhance the power of type systems, enabling robust and maintainable code.

Chapter 25

Primitive Data Types, Wrapper Classes

Primitive data types like `int`, `double`, and `char` cannot participate directly in Java's type hierarchy. Wrapper classes provide an object-oriented approach, wrapping primitive values into objects.

Example: Implementing a Simple Wrapper Class

```
package java.lang;

public class Integer {
    private final int value;

    public Integer(int value) {
```

```java
        this.value = value;
    }

    public int intValue() {
        return value;
    }
}
```

Using Wrapper Classes in a Container

```java
public class IntWrapperTest {
    public static void main(String[] args) {
        ObjectContainer oc = new ObjectContainer();
        oc.store(new Integer(1));
        Integer stored = (Integer) oc.get();
        System.out.println("Container contains: " +
        stored.intValue());
    }
}
```

Output:

```
Container contains: 1
```

25.1 Exercise 1: Manual Boxing

Write a program to manually wrap and unwrap a `double` value using its wrapper class `Double`. Then modify the program to use autoboxing and unboxing. Compare the outputs.

Solution: Manual Boxing Example

```
public class ManualBoxing {
    public static void main(String[] args) {
    // Manually wrapping:
        Double wrapped = new Double(3.14);
        // Manually unwrapping:
        double unwrapped = wrapped.doubleValue
        ();
        System.out.println("
        Manually boxed: " + wrapped);
        System.out.println("
        Manually unboxed: " + unwrapped);
    }
}
```

Output:

```
Manually boxed: 3.14
Manually unboxed: 3.14
```

Solution: Autoboxing Example

```
public class Autoboxing {
    public static void main(String[] args) {
        Double wrapped = 3.14; // Autoboxing
        double unwrapped = wrapped; // Unboxing
```

```
        System.out.println("Autoboxed: " +
        wrapped);
        System.out.println("Auto-unboxed: " +
        unwrapped);
    }
}
```

Output:

```
Autoboxed: 3.14
Auto-unboxed: 3.14
```

25.2 Autoboxing and Unboxing

Autoboxing and unboxing simplify working with wrapper classes. Here's an improved `WrapperTest` using autoboxing:

```
public class WrapperTest {
    public static void main(String[] args) {
        ObjectContainer oc = new
        ObjectContainer();
        oc.store(1); // Autoboxing
        int value = (Integer) oc.get();
        // Unboxing
        System.out.println("
        Container contains: " + value);
    }
}
```

Output:

```
Container contains: 1
```

Chapter 26

Arrays and Subtyping

Arrays in Java follow specific subtyping rules. If `S` is a subtype of `T`, then `S[]` is a subtype of `T[]`. However, this flexibility introduces potential risks.

Example: Valid Subtyping

```
// Valid because Dog is a subtype of Animal:
Animal[] animals = new Dog[2];
animals[0] = new Dog();
System.out.println("
Stored a Dog in the Animal array.");
```

Output:

```
Stored a Dog in the Animal array.
```

26.1 Exercise:

Create an **Animal** class and a **Dog** subclass. Attempt to assign a **Dog** object to an **Animal[]** array, then perform an invalid write operation.

Solution

```
class Animal {
    public void speak() {
        System.out.println("Animal speaks");
    }
}

class Dog extends Animal {
    @Override
    public void speak() {
        System.out.println("Dog barks");
    }
}

public class ArrayTest {
    public static void main(String[] args) {
    // Valid assignment:
        Animal[] animals = new Dog[2];
        animals[0] = new Dog(); // Valid
        try {
        // Causes ArrayStoreException:
            animals[1] = new Animal();
```

```
        } catch (ArrayStoreException e) {
            System.out.println("
            Caught ArrayStoreException: " +
            e.getMessage());
        }
    }
}
```

Output:

```
Caught ArrayStoreException:
java.lang.ArrayStoreException: Animal
```

Explanation: The runtime checks prevent an invalid `Animal` object from being stored in a `Dog[]`.

26.2 Summary

In this chapter, we explored:

- How wrapper classes enable subtyping for primitive data types.
- The convenience of autoboxing and unboxing.
- Array subtyping rules and how Java enforces type safety with runtime checks.

Chapter 27

Classification in Object-Oriented Programming

27.1 Introduction to Classification

Classification is a fundamental concept used to organize knowledge, objects, and their properties. In object-oriented programming, classification structures programs and libraries, improving clarity, modularity, and reusability. Examples include:

- **Exceptions**: Organized hierarchically, such as **IOException** and `NullPointerException`.
- **Streams**: Grouped into input/output classes, e.g., `FileInputStream`, `BufferedOutputStream`.

- **Graphical components**: Structured by types and events, such as buttons and their corresponding click events.

Classification provides an efficient way to understand and manipulate complex systems by relating objects through common properties.

27.2 Hierarchy in Classification

A good classification system organizes concepts in a hierarchy:

1. **General terms** are placed higher in the hierarchy than specific terms.
2. Every object of a specialized class is also an object of its general class.

For example:

- The term *Animal* is more general than *Dog*.
- In Java, the class **Exception** is more general than **ArithmeticException**.

Key Principle: General classes include all objects of their specialized subclasses. Specialized classes add specific properties while still conforming to their parent class.

27.3 The Is-A Relation

An effective classification system relies on the **is-a relationship**, meaning:

> *A is a B* implies A inherits all properties of B and may introduce additional properties.

For instance:

- A *Dog* is an *Animal* because it inherits all behaviors of an *Animal* and introduces dog-specific behaviors like barking.

27.3.1 Example: Is-A Relationship in Java

Listing 27.1: Is-A Relationship Example

```
class Animal {
    public void eat() {
        System.out.println("This animal eats food.");
    }
}

class Dog extends Animal {
    public void bark() {
        System.out.println("This dog barks.");
    }
}

```

```java
public class Main {
    public static void main(String[] args) {
        Animal myAnimal = new Animal();
        Dog myDog = new Dog();

        myAnimal.eat();
        // Outputs: This animal eats food.
        myDog.eat();
        // Outputs: This animal eats food.
        myDog.bark();
        // Outputs: This dog barks.
    }
}
```

27.3.2 Explanation

In this example:

- `Dog` is a subclass of `Animal`.
- The `eat` method is inherited by `Dog`, demonstrating the *is-a* relationship.
- The `bark` method is specific to `Dog`, showcasing specialization.

27.4 Interfaces and Class Hierarchies

Objects have clearly defined interfaces that specify which methods and attributes they provide. Classes and their objects can be classified by their interfaces:

- A class is **more specialized** if its interface includes attributes and methods of another class and adds additional properties.
- Special classes are *hierarchically below* general classes.

27.4.1 Example: Specialized Interfaces

Listing 27.2: Interface Hierarchies Example

```
interface Vehicle {
    void start();
}

class Car implements Vehicle {
    public void start() {
        System.out.println("Car is starting.");
    }

    public void openTrunk() {
        System.out.println("Trunk is open.");
    }
}

public class Main {
    public static void main(String[] args) {
        Vehicle myVehicle = new Car();
```

```
        myVehicle.start(); // Outputs: Car is starting.
        // myVehicle.openTrunk();
        // Error: Method not accessible from Vehicle.
    }
}
```

27.4.2 Explanation

- The Car class implements the Vehicle interface, inheriting the start method.
- When a Car object is referenced as a Vehicle, only the methods defined in the Vehicle interface are accessible.

27.5 Class and Type Hierarchies

Classifications in object-oriented programming are expressed using class and type hierarchies. Most languages provide a **most general type**:

- In Java, the Object class serves as the root of all classes.

This design allows for flexibility while maintaining a clear hierarchy. For example:

- A List<Object> can store any type of object.

- Casting and the **instanceof** operator can help manage more specific object types.

27.6 Exercises

Exercise 1

Explain why hierarchical classification is useful in programming. **Solution:** Hierarchical classification simplifies code reuse, reduces redundancy, and organizes relationships between objects, making systems easier to maintain and extend.

Exercise 2

Implement a `Bird` class with a `fly` method and a `Parrot` subclass that adds a `talk` method. **Solution:**

```
class Bird {
    public void fly() {
        System.out.println("This bird is flying.
        ");
    }
}

class Parrot extends Bird {
    public void talk() {
        System.out.println("This parrot is
        talking.");
    }
```

```
}

public class Main {
    public static void main(String[] args) {
        Bird myBird = new Bird();
        Parrot myParrot = new Parrot();

        myBird.fly();
        // Outputs: This bird is flying.
        myParrot.fly();
        // Outputs: This bird is flying.
        myParrot.talk();
        // Outputs: This parrot is talking.
    }
}
```

Exercise 3

Create an interface called `Playable` with a `play` method. Implement it in a `Guitar` class. Instantiate multiple objects in `main()` to demonstrate polymorphism. **Solution:**

```
interface Playable {
    void play();
}

class Guitar implements Playable {
    public void play() {
```

```
        System.out.println("Playing the guitar.
        ");
    }
}

public class Main {
    public static void main(String[] args) {
        Playable instrument = new Guitar();
        instrument.play();
        // Outputs: Playing the guitar.
    }
}
```

Chapter 28

Specialization in Object-Oriented Programming

28.1 Introduction to Specialization

Specialization is a cornerstone of object-oriented programming. It refers to refining or extending a class or type by adding more specific properties or behaviors. The dual concept to specialization is *abstraction*, which focuses on generalizing types. This chapter focuses on specialization, while abstraction will be discussed in the following chapter.

Specialization allows us to adapt existing classes to new requirements, reducing the need for redundant code. For example, frameworks and toolkits in Java are built to provide general functionality, which can be specialized to meet specific needs. This concept is closely tied to inheritance, which we explore in detail here.

28.2 Inheritance for Specialization

Inheritance is the primary mechanism in object-oriented programming for specialization. By extending a base class, you can inherit its properties and behaviors while adding or overriding specific features to cater to more specialized use cases.

Advantages of inheritance include:

- **Code Reusability:** Avoid duplication by inheriting standard properties and methods from a base class.
- **Encapsulation:** Reuse functionality without needing to expose or understand the base class's implementation.
- **Interoperability:** Inherited functionality can include code written in other languages or precompiled binaries.

Example: Specializing a Number Container

Consider the following example, where we extend a 'NumberContainer' class to track the maximum value stored.

```
// Base class: NumberContainer
public class NumberContainer {
    private Number element;

    public void store(Number element) {
        this.element = element;
    }

    public Number get() {
        return element;
    }
}

// Specialized class:
NumberContainerWithMaximum
public class NumberContainerWithMaximum
extends NumberContainer {
    private Number maximum;

    @Override
    public void store(Number element) {
        super.store(element);
        if (maximum == null ||
        element.doubleValue() >
        maximum.doubleValue()) {
            maximum = element;
        }
    }
```

```

    public Number getMaximum() {
        return maximum;
    }

    public void clearMaximum() {
        maximum = null;
    }
}
```

Explanation

- The 'NumberContainer' class provides basic storage functionality for a single number. - The 'NumberContainerWithMaximum' class extends this functionality by tracking the maximum value stored. - The 'store' method is overridden to update the 'maximum' field whenever a new value is added. - A new method, 'clearMaximum', resets the maximum value.

Test Class

```
public class TestNumberContainer {
    public static void main(String[] args) {
        NumberContainerWithMaximum container =
        new NumberContainerWithMaximum();
        container.store(15);
        container.store(30);
        container.store(20);
```

```
        System.out.println("Stored number: " +
        container.get()); // Expected: 20
        System.out.println("Maximum number: " +
        container.getMaximum()); // Expected:
        30

        container.clearMaximum();
        System.out.println("Maximum cleared.");
        System.out.println("Stored number: " +
        container.get()); // Expected: 20
        System.out.println("Maximum number: " +
        container.getMaximum()); // Expected:
        null
    }
}
```

Expected Output

```
Stored number: 20
Maximum number: 30
Maximum cleared.
Stored number: 20
Maximum number: null
```

28.3 Subtyping and Subclassing in Java

In Java, subclassing implies subtyping, meaning that an instance of a subclass can be used wherever an instance of its superclass is expected. This behavior is fundamental to type systems in object-oriented programming.

The **Liskov Substitution Principle (LSP)** dictates that objects of a subclass must be usable in place of objects of the superclass without altering the correctness of the program. Violations of this principle often lead to unexpected behavior.

Example: Violating LSP

```
public class Rectangle {
    protected int width, height;

    public void setWidth(int width) {
        this.width = width;
    }

    public void setHeight(int height) {
        this.height = height;
    }

    public int area() {
        return width * height;
    }
```

```
}

public class Square extends Rectangle {
    @Override
    public void setWidth(int width) {
        super.setWidth(width);
        super.setHeight(width);
    }

    @Override
    public void setHeight(int height) {
        super.setWidth(height);
        super.setHeight(height);
    }
}
```

Issue

The 'Square' class overrides the 'setWidth' and 'setHeight' methods to maintain its invariant (equal width and height). However, this breaks LSP because the 'Square' does not behave consistently with the 'Rectangle' contract.

Solution: Avoiding LSP Violations

```
public interface Shape {
    void setWidth(int width);
    void setHeight(int height);
```

```
    int area();
}

public class Rectangle implements Shape {
    protected int width, height;

    @Override
    public void setWidth(int width) {
        this.width = width;
    }

    @Override
    public void setHeight(int height) {
        this.height = height;
    }

    @Override
    public int area() {
        return width * height;
    }
}

public class Square implements Shape {
    private int side;

    @Override
    public void setWidth(int width) {
        this.side = width;
    }
```

```

    @Override
    public void setHeight(int height) {
        this.side = height;
    }

    @Override
    public int area() {
        return side * side;
    }
}
```

Test Class and Output

```
public class TestShapes {
    public static void main(String[] args) {
        Shape rectangle = new Rectangle();
        rectangle.setWidth(4);
        rectangle.setHeight(5);
        System.out.println("Rectangle area: " +
        rectangle.area()); // Expected: 20

        Shape square = new Square();
        square.setWidth(4);
        square.setHeight(5);
        // Dimensions mismatch intentionally
        System.out.println("Square area: " +
        square.area()); // Expected: 16
    }
```

```
}
```

```
Rectangle area: 20
Square area: 16
```

28.4 Boxing and Unboxing in Java

Boxing occurs when a primitive type (e.g., **int**, **double**) is automatically converted to its wrapper class (e.g., `Integer`, `Double`) to satisfy a method or type requirement. Unboxing is the reverse operation, converting a wrapper class to its corresponding primitive type.

28.4.1 Modified NumberContainerWithMaximum

Below is a modified version of the NumberContainerWithMaximum class, designed to work explicitly with **int** values. The class demonstrates how boxing and unboxing are seamlessly handled by Java.

```java
// Modified NumberContainerWithMaximum
public class NumberContainerWithMaximum {
    private Number element;
    private Number maximum;

    public void store(int value) {
    // Boxing: primitive int to Integer (
    Number)
```

```
    this.element = value;
    if (maximum == null ||
    value > maximum.intValue()) {
        // Unboxing: maximum (Number) to int
        this.maximum = value;
        }
    }

    public Number get() {
        return element;
    }

    public Number getMaximum() {
        return maximum;
    }

    public void clearMaximum() {
        this.maximum = null;
    }
}
```

28.4.2 Test Class for Boxing and Unboxing

The following test class demonstrates how boxing and unboxing work in practice. The output confirms the correctness of the operations.

```
// Test class for Boxing and Unboxing
public class TestBoxingUnboxing {
    public static void main(String[] args) {
```

```
        NumberContainerWithMaximum container =
        new NumberContainerWithMaximum();

        // Store values
        container.store(15); // Boxing: int -> Number
        container.store(30); // Boxing: int -> Number
        container.store(20); // Boxing: int -> Number

        // Retrieve stored values
        System.out.println("Stored number: " +
        container.get()); // Unboxing: Number -> int
        System.out.println("Maximum number: " +
        container.getMaximum());
        // Unboxing: Number -> int

        // Clear maximum
        container.clearMaximum();
        System.out.println("Maximum cleared.");
        System.out.println("Maximum number: " +
        container.getMaximum()); // Should be null

        // Add a new value
        container.store(10);
        System.out.println("Stored number: " +
```

```
        container.get());
        System.out.println("Maximum number: " +
        container.getMaximum());
        // Unboxing: Should match the last
        stored value
    }
}
```

28.4.3 Expected Output

When the above test class is executed, the following output is produced:

```
Stored number: 20
Maximum number: 30
Maximum cleared.
Maximum number: null
Stored number: 10
Maximum number: 10
```

28.4.4 Explanations of Boxing and Unboxing

- **Boxing:**
  - Occurs in `store(int value)` when the `int` value is assigned to the `Number` field (`this.element` and `this.maximum`).
  - Java automatically converts the primitive `int` to an `Integer` object (a subclass of `Number`).

- **Unboxing:**
  - Happens when comparing `value` with `maximum.intValue()` in the `store` method.
  - The `intValue()` method converts the `Number` (wrapper) back into a primitive `int` for comparison.
  - Also occurs implicitly when retrieving and printing the `maximum` field using `getMaximum()` in the `main` method.

This section highlights the ease with which Java handles primitive types and their wrapper classes, making boxing and unboxing powerful tools for efficient programming.

—

The chapter has been crafted to provide a thorough exploration of specialization, inheritance, and related concepts like subtyping, LSP, and boxing/unboxing. Each example, explanation, and exercise reinforces the theoretical foundations and practical applications of specialization in Java.

Chapter 29

Abstraction and Interfaces in Java

Introduction to Abstraction and Interfaces

Abstraction, or generalization, is a key concept in object-oriented programming. It enables us to express specific abilities of objects as a type of their own, without needing to specify exactly how these abilities are realized. This is particularly useful in scenarios where multiple developers collaborate on a program. Abstraction extracts the essential details and omits the unnecessary.

For instance, consider various real-life objects, each with a weight. These objects belong to different classes, making it impractical to organize them in a meaningful hierarchy. Since the Java `Object` class does not have a `getWeight()` method, we cannot uniformly request the weight of such objects without defining this method repeatedly in every class. In more general terms, an interface helps to summarize properties that several unrelated classes can still have in common, such as a specific method like `getWeight`. By defining these shared properties at the interface level, we enable diverse classes to adhere to a common contract, promoting uniformity and simplifying code design.

Using abstraction, we can define a common interface type that all such objects adhere to. This allows us to treat them uniformly while still maintaining their unique implementations.

29.1 Defining Interfaces

An interface in Java defines a contract that classes can implement. Interfaces do not provide method implementations, making them inherently abstract. A class declares that it implements an interface using the `implements` keyword.

For example:

```
public interface Weighable {
    double getWeight();
}
```

Here, `Weighable` is an interface, defining the contract that any class implementing it must provide a getWeight() method.

29.2 Using Interfaces

Consider the following classes:

```
public class Animal implements Weighable {
    private double weight;

    public Animal(double weight) {
        this.weight = weight;
    }

    @Override
    public double getWeight() {
        return weight;
    }
}

public class Apple implements Weighable {
    private double weight;

    public Apple(double weight) {
        this.weight = weight;
    }

    @Override
    public double getWeight() {
        return weight;
    }
```

```
}
```

Both `Animal` and `Apple` implement the `Weighable` interface by defining the `getWeight()` method. This allows us to treat objects of these classes as `Weighable`.

29.3 The `MaxWeightContainer` Class

Using the `Weighable` interface, we can define a container class that holds the heaviest object:

```
public class MaxWeightContainer {
    private Weighable heaviest;

    public void store(Weighable element) {
        if (heaviest == null ||
        element.getWeight() > heaviest.
        getWeight()) {
            heaviest = element;
        }
    }

    public Weighable getHeaviest() {
        return heaviest;
    }
}
```

29.4 Example Usage

Here's an example program that demonstrates how to use the **MaxWeightContainer** class:

```
public class Main {
    public static void main(String[] args) {
        MaxWeightContainer container =
        new MaxWeightContainer();

        Animal dog = new Animal(30.0);
        Apple apple = new Apple(1.2);

        container.store(dog);
        container.store(apple);

        System.out.println("Heaviest object
        weight: " +
                container.getHeaviest().
                getWeight());
    }
}
```

Output:

```
Heaviest object weight: 30.0
```

29.5 Key Notes About Interfaces

- An interface is a supertype of all classes that implement it.

- Interfaces do not implement methods; they only define the method signatures.
- Interfaces are inherently abstract, and you cannot instantiate them.
- Every object that implements an interface is an instance of its implementing class.
- Interfaces can define constants (fields declared as **public static final**).
- Interfaces define the presence of methods but do not provide implementations, leaving it to the implementing classes to define the specific behavior of those methods.

29.6 Exercises

Exercise 1

Define a new class `Book` that implements the `Weighable` interface. Create several `Book` objects and test them with the `MaxWeightContainer` class.

Solution:

```
public class Book implements Weighable {
    private double weight;

    public Book(double weight) {
        this.weight = weight;
```

```
    }

    @Override
    public double getWeight() {
        return weight;
    }
}

public class Main {
    public static void main(String[] args) {
        MaxWeightContainer container =
        new MaxWeightContainer();

        Book book1 = new Book(2.5);
        Book book2 = new Book(3.8);

        container.store(book1);
        container.store(book2);

        System.out.println("Heaviest book
        weight: " +
                container.getHeaviest().
                getWeight());
    }
}
```

Output:

```
Heaviest book weight: 3.8
```

Exercise 2

Extend the `Weighable` interface to include a method `getName()`. Update the `MaxWeightContainer` class to display the name of the heaviest object. Provide examples and test cases.

Solution:

```
public interface Weighable {
    double getWeight();
    String getName();
}

public class Animal implements Weighable {
    private double weight;
    private String name;

    public Animal(String name, double weight) {
        this.name = name;
        this.weight = weight;
    }

    @Override
    public double getWeight() {
        return weight;
    }

    @Override
    public String getName() {
```

```
        return name;
    }
}

public class Main {
    public static void main(String[] args) {
        MaxWeightContainer container =
        new MaxWeightContainer();

        Animal dog = new Animal("Dog", 30.0);
        Animal cat = new Animal("Cat", 15.0);

        container.store(dog);
        container.store(cat);

        Weighable heaviest = container.
        getHeaviest();
        System.out.println("Heaviest object: "
        +
                heaviest.getName() + " with
                weight " +
                heaviest.getWeight());
    }
}
```

Output:

```
Heaviest object: Dog with weight 30.0
```

29.7 Conclusion

Interfaces in Java are a powerful tool for abstraction. They allow us to define contracts that classes can implement, enabling code reuse, flexibility, and clear design. Through abstraction, we can generalize common behaviors while preserving individual implementations. Every object in object-oriented programming has a clearly defined interface that specifies its methods and attributes. These interfaces enable the classification of objects, forming a foundation for structured program design. More general objects are characterized by smaller, more abstract interfaces, while specialized objects expand on these interfaces with additional attributes and methods. Through classification and specialization, we can define and implement types systematically, often inheriting implementation details to enhance reusability. Abstraction complements this by summarizing common properties across different types, allowing us to reduce and generalize interfaces while maintaining flexibility and cohesion.

Chapter 30

Classification and Subtyping

30.1 Introduction

In object-oriented programming, *classification* and *subtyping* are essential tools for creating flexible and reusable systems. A significant design decision involves determining whether certain types should be implemented as *classes*, *interfaces*, or *abstract classes*. This chapter explores this decision-making process using a practical example and provides guidelines for when to use each construct.

Definition of an Abstract Class

An **abstract class** in Java is a class that cannot be instantiated directly because it is incomplete. It is designed to serve as a base for other classes to extend and must be declared using the `abstract` keyword. Abstract classes can have:

- **Abstract Methods**: Methods declared without a body (implementation). These methods must be implemented by subclasses. For example:

```
public abstract class Shape {
    public abstract double getArea();
}
```

- **Concrete Methods**: Methods with complete implementations that can be inherited by subclasses. For example:

```
public abstract class Animal {
    public void eat() {
        System.out.println("
        This animal eats food.");
    }
}
```

- **Attributes**: Variables that subclasses inherit and may override or extend.

An abstract class bridges the gap between fully implemented classes and completely abstract interfaces. It allows developers to define shared behavior (methods or attributes) while enforcing that specific details be provided by subclasses.

30.2 The Example Scenario

Consider the following types:

- `Dog`
- `Object`
- `Parcel`
- `Weighable`
- `PostalItem`
- `Letter`
- `PDFDocument`
- `Printable`

The relationships between these types are as follows:

- `Dogs`, `Parcels`, and `Letters` can be weighed.
- `Parcels` and `Letters` can be sent via post.
- `Letters` and `PDFDocuments` can be printed.

Exercise for the Reader: Based on this information, try to construct a type hierarchy that reflects these relationships. Think about which types should be declared as classes, interfaces or abstract classes. Additionally, implement meaningful methods for each class and define suitable attributes where appropriate.

30.3 Guiding Principles for Design

When deciding whether to implement a type as a class, interface, or abstract class, consider the following guidelines:

30.3.1 When to Use Interfaces

If a type is highly abstract or defines only behavior without committing to any implementation details, it is best to use an interface. This is particularly relevant when:

- You want to define a contract for multiple unrelated classes to adhere to.
- A type is higher in the type hierarchy and serves as a general abstraction.
- A type needs to have multiple supertypes (Java allows multiple interface inheritance).

For instance, in our scenario:

Interfaces, Abstract Classes, Concrete Classes

Interfaces

`Weighable`

```
public interface Weighable {
    double getWeight();
}
```

Explanation: This interface represents the ability to weigh an object. Since weighing is a common property across very different entities (like dogs, parcels, and letters), it's defined as an interface. This allows any class that can be weighed to implement it, regardless of its place in the hierarchy.

`Printable`

```
public interface Printable {
    void print();
}
```

Explanation: This interface captures the ability to print an object. Since printing is a behavior shared by unrelated entities (like letters and PDF documents), defining it as an interface ensures flexibility and avoids limiting the design by tying it to a specific class hierarchy.

Abstract Classes

30.3.2 When to Use Abstract Classes

Abstract classes are suitable when a type lies between full abstraction and full implementation. Use them when:

- You want to define common behavior for subclasses while leaving some methods abstract.
- You need to share attributes or partially implemented methods among related classes.

For instance, in our scenario:

PostalItem

```
public abstract class PostalItem implements Weighable {
    private String recipientAddress;

    public PostalItem(String recipientAddress) {
        this.recipientAddress = recipientAddress;
    }

    public String getRecipientAddress() {
        return recipientAddress;
    }

```

```
    public abstract void send();
}
```

Explanation:

- **Why an abstract class?** A `PostalItem` is a concept that applies only to objects like parcels and letters, which have additional behaviors (e.g., sending). By making it abstract, we ensure that no generic `PostalItem` object can be created—it's meant to serve as a base for more specific types.

- **Attributes and common behavior:** The `recipientAddress` is common to all `PostalItem` types and is declared in the abstract class to avoid redundancy. Similarly, the `getRecipientAddress()` method provides shared functionality.

- **Abstract methods:** The `send()` method is abstract because its implementation depends on the specific type of postal item (e.g., a letter might involve different logistics than a parcel).

Concrete Classes

30.3.3 When to Use Classes

If a type represents a concrete object or contains implementation details, it is better to use a class. This is especially true when:

- The type has no further subtypes.
- You want to define attributes and implementation details for methods.

For instance, in our scenario:

Parcel

```
public class Parcel extends PostalItem {
    private double weight;

    public Parcel(String recipientAddress,
    double weight) {
        super(recipientAddress);
        this.weight = weight;
    }

    @Override
    public double getWeight() {
        return weight;
    }

    @Override
    public void send() {
        System.out.println("Parcel sent to: " +
        getRecipientAddress());
    }
}
```

Explanation: A `Parcel` is a concrete type of `PostalItem`. It:

- **Implements the Weighable interface:**
  By extending **PostalItem**, it inherits the contract of **Weighable** and must implement the **getWeight()** method.

- **Specializes the `send()` method:** The behavior for sending a parcel is defined here, as it's specific to this type.

`Letter`

```
public class Letter extends PostalItem
implements Printable {
    private double weight;

    public Letter(String recipientAddress,
    double weight) {
        super(recipientAddress);
        this.weight = weight;
    }

    @Override
    public double getWeight() {
        return weight;
    }

    @Override
```

```
    public void send() {
        System.out.println("Letter sent to: " +
        getRecipientAddress());
    }

    @Override
    public void print() {
        System.out.println("Printing the letter
        ...");
    }
}
```

Explanation: A `Letter` is another concrete type of `PostalItem` with some additional capabilities:

- **Implements `Printable`:**
  Letters can be printed, so the `print()` method is provided.

- **Implements `Weighable`:** Like all `PostalItem` objects, letters can be weighed.

- **Specializes `send()` method:** The behavior for sending a letter is defined here.

`PDFDocument`

```
public class PDFDocument implements Printable
{
    private String content;

```

```
    public PDFDocument(String content) {
        this.content = content;
    }

    @Override
    public void print() {
        System.out.println("
        Printing PDF Document: " + content);
    }
}
```

Explanation: A `PDFDocument`:

- **Implements `Printable`:** It is unrelated to `PostalItem` but shares the ability to be printed.
- **Standalone entity:** Since it's not part of the postal hierarchy, it doesn't extend `PostalItem` or implement `Weighable`.

Dog

```
public class Dog implements Weighable {
    private double weight;

    public Dog(double weight) {
        this.weight = weight;
    }

    @Override
```

```
    public double getWeight() {
        return weight;
    }
}
```

Explanation: A `Dog`:

- **Implements `Weighable`:** It has a weight property but is not part of the `PostalItem` hierarchy.
- **Standalone entity:** This class showcases the flexibility of using an interface, as `Dog` can implement `Weighable` independently of the postal types.

Testing the Hierarchy

```
public class Main {
    public static void main(String[] args) {
        // Create objects
        Parcel parcel =
        new Parcel("123 Elm Street", 10.5);
        Letter letter =
        new Letter("456 Oak Avenue", 1.2);
        PDFDocument pdf =
        new PDFDocument("Document Content");
        Dog dog = new Dog(25.0);

        // Test Printable
        letter.print();
        pdf.print();
```

```

        // Test Weighable
        System.out.println("Dog weight: " +
        dog.getWeight() + " kg");
        System.out.println("Parcel weight: " +
        parcel.getWeight() + " kg");

        // Test PostalItem
        parcel.send();
        letter.send();
    }
}
```

Explanation: This `Main` class demonstrates how the objects interact with their interfaces and superclasses. It:

1. **Tests interface methods:** Calls `print()` for `Printable` objects and `getWeight()` for `Weighable` objects.

2. **Verifies abstract class behavior:** Uses the `send()` method defined in the `PostalItem` subclasses.

3. **Shows flexibility:**
Highlights how unrelated types (`Dog`, `PDFDocument`) can coexist in the same program because of shared interfaces.

30.4 Advantages of Proper Classification

Choosing the right constructs enhances software design by:

- Encouraging code reuse through shared behavior and attributes.
- Promoting flexibility and maintainability by abstracting commonalities.
- Allowing multiple inheritance of behavior using interfaces.

30.5 Conclusion

In object-oriented design, the relationship between classification and subtyping is pivotal for organizing and structuring software. Interfaces provide a way to define shared behavior without implementation, classes represent concrete realizations of types, and abstract classes serve as a bridge between the two. By carefully considering the role of each type in your hierarchy, you can create systems that are both robust and extensible.

Chapter 31

Parameterization of Types

31.1 Introduction to Type Parameterization

Type parameterization, also known as generics in Java, is a powerful feature that enables defining classes, interfaces, and methods with type placeholders. This promotes flexibility, reusability, and type safety in programming. By parameterizing types, we avoid the need for casting and reduce the risk of runtime errors.

31.2 Parameterized Classes

A parameterized class uses a type parameter to specify the type of its fields, methods, or constructors. The type parameter is denoted by a single uppercase letter, commonly `T` for "type."

31.2.1 Example: Generic Box Class

The following example demonstrates a generic `Box` class that can store objects of any type:

```java
class Box<T> {
    private T content;

    public void setContent(T content) {
        this.content = content;
    }

    public T getContent() {
        return content;
    }

    public static void main(String[] args) {
        Box<String> stringBox = new Box<>();
        stringBox.setContent("Hello, Generics!");
        System.out.println(stringBox.getContent());

```

```java
        Box<Integer> intBox = new Box<>();
        intBox.setContent(42);
        System.out.println(intBox.getContent());
    }
}
```

Explanation

In this example:

- The `Box<T>` class has a type parameter `T`, representing the type of the content it holds.
- The `main` method demonstrates how the `Box` class can be instantiated with different types, such as `String` and `Integer`.
- The program outputs:

```
Hello, Generics!
42
```

31.3 Parameterized Interfaces

Interfaces can also be parameterized to define methods that work with various types.

31.3.1 Example: Generic Repository Interface

```java
interface Repository<T> {
    void save(T entity);
    T findById(int id);
}
class UserRepository implements Repository<String> {
    @Override
    public void save(String user) {
        System.out.println("User saved: " + user);
    }

    @Override
    public String findById(int id) {
        return "User" + id;
    }

    public static void main(String[] args) {
        Repository<String> userRepo =
        new UserRepository();
        userRepo.save("Alice");
        System.out.println(userRepo.findById(1));
    }
}
```

Explanation

- The `Repository<T>` interface defines generic methods for saving and retrieving entities.
- The `UserRepository` class implements this interface with `String` as the type parameter.
- The program outputs:

```
User saved: Alice
User1
```

31.4 Bounded Type Parameters

Type parameters can be restricted using bounds. This ensures that only types meeting certain criteria can be used.

31.4.1 Example: Bounded Type Parameter

```java
class NumberBox<T extends Number> {
    private T number;

    public void setNumber(T number) {
        this.number = number;
    }

    public double getDoubleValue() {
        return number.doubleValue();
```

```java
    }

    public static void main(String[] args) {
        NumberBox<Integer> intBox = new NumberBox<>();
        intBox.setNumber(42);
        System.out.println(intBox.getDoubleValue());

        NumberBox<Double> doubleBox =
        new NumberBox<>();
        doubleBox.setNumber(3.14);
        System.out.println(doubleBox.getDoubleValue());
    }
}
```

Explanation

- The `NumberBox<T>` class restricts `T` to subclasses of `Number`, such as `Integer` and `Double`.
- The program outputs:

```
42.0
3.14
```

31.5 Exercises

1. Define a generic class `Pair<T, U>` that can hold two objects of potentially different types. Implement methods to set and retrieve each object.

2. Extend the `NumberBox<T>` class to include a method `add(NumberBox<T> other)` that adds the values of two `NumberBox` objects and returns the result.

3. Implement a generic method `swap(T[] array, int i, int j)` that swaps two elements in an array.

31.5.1 Exercise Solutions

Solution to Exercise 1

```
class Pair<T, U> {
    private T first;
    private U second;

    public void setFirst(T first) {
        this.first = first;
    }

    public void setSecond(U second) {
        this.second = second;
    }
```

```

    public T getFirst() {
        return first;
    }

    public U getSecond() {
        return second;
    }

    public static void main(String[] args) {
        Pair<String, Integer> pair = new Pair
        <>();
        pair.setFirst("Hello");
        pair.setSecond(42);
        System.out.println(pair.getFirst() +
        " " + pair.getSecond());
    }
}
```

Output:

```
Hello 42
```

Solution to Exercise 2

```
class NumberBox<T extends Number> {
    private T number;

    public void setNumber(T number) {
        this.number = number;
```

```
    }

    public double getDoubleValue() {
        return number.doubleValue();
    }

    public NumberBox<T> add(NumberBox<T> other)
     {
        NumberBox<T> result = new NumberBox<>()
        ;
        result.setNumber(
        (T) Double.valueOf(this.getDoubleValue
        () +
        other.getDoubleValue()));
        return result;
    }

    public static void main(String[] args) {
        NumberBox<Double> box1 = new NumberBox
        <>();
        box1.setNumber(3.14);
        NumberBox<Double> box2 = new NumberBox
        <>();
        box2.setNumber(2.71);

        NumberBox<Double> sumBox = box1.add(
        box2);
        System.out.println(sumBox.
        getDoubleValue());
```

```
    }
}
```

Output:

```
5.85
```

Solution to Exercise 3

```
class ArrayUtils {
    public static <T> void swap(
    T[] array, int i, int j) {
        T temp = array[i];
        array[i] = array[j];
        array[j] = temp;
    }

    public static void main(String[] args) {
        String[] words =
        {"Java", "Generics", "Example"};
        swap(words, 0, 2);
        for (String word : words) {
            System.out.print(word + " ");
        }
    }
}
```

Output:

```
Example Generics Java
```

Chapter 32

Polymorphism

32.1 Introduction to Polymorphism

Polymorphism, derived from the Greek words **poly** (many) and **morph** (forms), is one of the core principles of object-oriented programming (OOP). It enables objects to take on many forms, providing flexibility in how code is written and extended.

There are two main types of polymorphism:

- **Compile-Time Polymorphism (Ad-hoc Polymorphism)**: Resolved during compilation, often achieved through method overloading.

- **Runtime Polymorphism (Subtype Polymorphism)**: Resolved at runtime, typically via method overriding in inheritance.

Polymorphism promotes code reusability and extensibility, making it easier to build scalable systems.

32.2 Types of Polymorphism

32.2.1 Subtype Polymorphism

Subtype polymorphism is achieved through inheritance, where a parent class reference can hold child class objects. This is the foundation of dynamic method dispatch in Java.

Example:

```
interface Vehicle {
    void startEngine();
}

class Car implements Vehicle {
    @Override
    public void startEngine() {
        System.out.println("Car engine started!
            ");
    }
}

class Bike implements Vehicle {
    @Override
    public void startEngine() {
        System.out.println("Bike engine started
            !");
```

```
    }
}

public class SubtypeExample {
    public static void main(String[] args) {
        Vehicle vehicle1 = new Car();
        Vehicle vehicle2 = new Bike();

        vehicle1.startEngine();
        // Output: Car engine started!
        vehicle2.startEngine();
        // Output: Bike engine started!
    }
}
```

32.2.2 Parameterized Polymorphism

Enabled by generics, parameterized polymorphism allows writing flexible and type-safe code by parameterizing types.

Example:

```
class Container<T> {
    private T item;

    public void setItem(T item) {
        this.item = item;
    }

    public T getItem() {
```

```
        return item;
    }
}

public class ParameterizedExample {
    public static void main(String[] args) {
        Container<String> stringContainer =
        new Container<>();
        stringContainer.setItem("Hello");
        System.out.println("String in container
        : " +
        stringContainer.getItem());
        // Output: Hello

        Container<Integer> integerContainer =
        new Container<>();
        integerContainer.setItem(42);
        System.out.println("Integer in
        container: " +
        integerContainer.getItem());
        // Output: 42
    }
}
```

32.2.3 Limited Parameter Polymorphism

This type restricts generic types with bounds, ensuring flexibility without losing type safety.

Example:

```java
import java.util.List;

public class BoundedGenerics {
    public static
    <T extends Number>
    double calculateSum(
    List<T> numbers) {
        double sum = 0.0;
        for (T number : numbers) {
            sum += number.doubleValue();
        }
        return sum;
    }

    public static void main(String[] args) {
        List<Integer> integers = List.of(1, 2,
        3, 4);
        System.out.println("Sum: " +
        calculateSum(integers));
        // Output: Sum: 10.0

        List<Double> doubles = List.of(1.1,
        2.2, 3.3);
        System.out.println("Sum: " +
        calculateSum(doubles));
        // Output: Sum: 6.6
    }
}
```

32.2.4 Ad-hoc Polymorphism

Ad-hoc polymorphism is achieved through method overloading or operator overloading (in languages that support it).

Example:

```
class AdHocExample {
    public int add(int a, int b) {
        return a + b;
    }

    public String add(String a, String b) {
        return a + b;
    }

    public static void main(String[] args) {
        AdHocExample example = new AdHocExample();

        System.out.println("Integer addition: " +
        example.add(2, 3)); // Output: 5
        System.out.println("String concatenation: " +
        example.add("Hello", " World"));
        // Output: Hello World
    }
}
```

32.3 Dynamic Method Dispatch

Dynamic method dispatch refers to the runtime resolution of overridden methods in inheritance.

Example:

```java
abstract class Animal {
    abstract void makeSound();
}

class Dog extends Animal {
    @Override
    void makeSound() {
        System.out.println("Woof!");
    }
}

class Cat extends Animal {
    @Override
    void makeSound() {
        System.out.println("Meow!");
    }
}

public class DynamicDispatchExample {
    public static void main(String[] args) {
        Animal animal = new Dog();
        animal.makeSound(); // Output: Woof!

        animal = new Cat();
```

```
        animal.makeSound(); // Output: Meow!
    }
}
```

32.4 Exercises and Solutions

Exercise 1: Subtype Polymorphism Create an interface `Appliance` with methods `turnOn` and `turnOff`. Implement subclasses `Fan` and `LightBulb`. Write a main program to demonstrate switching appliances on and off.

Solution:

```
interface Appliance {
    void turnOn();
    void turnOff();
}

class Fan implements Appliance {
    @Override
    public void turnOn() {
        System.out.println("Fan is now ON.");
    }

    @Override
    public void turnOff() {
        System.out.println("Fan is now OFF.");
    }
}

```

```
class LightBulb implements Appliance {
    @Override
    public void turnOn() {
        System.out.println("Light bulb is now
        ON.");
    }

    @Override
    public void turnOff() {
        System.out.println("Light bulb is now
        OFF.");
    }
}

public class ApplianceDemo {
    public static void main(String[] args) {
        Appliance fan = new Fan();
        Appliance bulb = new LightBulb();

        fan.turnOn();
        // Output: Fan is now ON.
        fan.turnOff();
        // Output: Fan is now OFF.
        bulb.turnOn();
        // Output: Light bulb is now ON.
        bulb.turnOff();
        // Output: Light bulb is now OFF.
    }
}
```

Exercise 2: Parameterized Polymorphism Write a class `Pair<T>` that holds two items of type `T`. Provide methods to set and get the items, and demonstrate how this class can hold different types of objects.

Solution:

```
class Pair<T> {
    private T first;
    private T second;

    public void setFirst(T first) {
        this.first = first;
    }

    public void setSecond(T second) {
        this.second = second;
    }

    public T getFirst() {
        return first;
    }

    public T getSecond() {
        return second;
    }

    public static void main(String[] args) {
        Pair<String> stringPair = new Pair<>();
        stringPair.setFirst("Hello");
        stringPair.setSecond("World");
```

```
        System.out.println("First: " +
        stringPair.getFirst());
        // Output: Hello
        System.out.println("Second: " +
        stringPair.getSecond());
        // Output: World

        Pair<Integer> intPair =
        new Pair<>();
        intPair.setFirst(1);
        intPair.setSecond(2);
        System.out.println("First: " +
        intPair.getFirst());
        // Output: 1
        System.out.println("Second: " +
        intPair.getSecond());
        // Output: 2
    }
}
```

Expected Output:

```
First: Hello
Second: World
First: 1
Second: 2
```

Exercise 3: Limited Parameterized Polymorphism Write a method that computes the product of a list of numbers using generics bounded by `Number`.

Solution:

```java
import java.util.List;

public class BoundedGenericsExample {
    public static <T extends Number>
    double calculateProduct(List<T> numbers) {
        double product = 1.0;
        for (T number : numbers) {
            product *= number.doubleValue();
        }
        return product;
    }

    public static void main(String[] args) {
        List<Integer> integers =
        List.of(1, 2, 3, 4);
        System.out.println("Product: " +
        calculateProduct(integers));
        // Output: Product: 24.0

        List<Double> doubles = List.of(1.1,
        2.0, 3.0);
        System.out.println("Product: " +
        calculateProduct(doubles));
        // Output: Product: 6.6
    }
}
```

Expected Output:

```
Product: 24.0
```

```
Product: 6.6
```

Exercise 4: Ad-hoc Polymorphism Create a method `print` that accepts either an integer or a string. Use method overloading to implement this.

Solution:

```java
public class AdHocPolymorphism {
    public void print(int num) {
        System.out.println("Integer: " + num);
    }

    public void print(String str) {
        System.out.println("String: " + str);
    }

    public static void main(String[] args) {
        AdHocPolymorphism adHoc =
        new AdHocPolymorphism();
        adHoc.print(42);
        // Output: Integer: 42
        adHoc.print("Hello");
        // Output: String: Hello
    }
}
```

Chapter 33

Final Word

Thank you for taking the time to explore this book. I hope it has provided you with a strong foundation in programming and equipped you with the confidence to delve deeper into the world of software development. Whether you're a beginner just starting out or someone expanding your knowledge, your commitment to learning is commendable.

If you have questions or feedback, or if you'd simply like to share your thoughts, feel free to reach out. I'd love to hear from you and assist where I can.

33.1 A Glimpse Into More Learning Opportunities

This book is part of a broader vision to provide you with resources that seamlessly complement one another:

1. Logic

My book on logic explores foundational and advanced logical systems, making concepts accessible for beginners while also covering formal topics like category theory, homotopy theory, and non-classical logics such as fuzzy logic and temporal logic. It's a perfect companion for understanding the theoretical underpinnings of programming and computation.

33.1.1 2. Advanced Basic Programming Skills

Soon, I'll release a follow-up to this book that dives deeper into essential programming concepts:

- Software modules and frameworks for building scalable applications.
- Parallel programming and distributed computing to tackle modern computational challenges.

This book will build on the knowledge you've gained here and prepare you for the next level of development skills.

33.1.2 3. Algorithms and Data Structures

Mastery of algorithms and data structures is crucial for writing efficient and effective programs. This upcoming book will guide you through the fundamental techniques and advanced methods, with clear explanations, practical examples, and exercises to hone your skills.

33.1.3 4. Theory of Computation and Complexity Theory

To deepen your understanding of what can and cannot be computed, as well as how to estimate the feasibility and efficiency of programs, these books cover:

- Computability: Exploring the limits of what programs can achieve.
- Automata Theory: Understanding abstract machines and their capabilities.
- Formal Languages: Learning how languages define the structure of computation.
- Complexity: Assessing the efficiency and feasibility of algorithms.

This book will empower you to evaluate program feasibility and optimize computational tasks.

33.1.4 Search, Sorting and Graph Algorithms

These textbooks focus on elementary and advanced algorithms for searching, sorting, and graph processing. Topics covered include linear and binary search; comparison-based sorting algorithms (Quicksort, Mergesort, Heapsort); non-comparison-based sorting (Radix); search structures (hashing, trees, heaps); and graph algorithms (BFS, DFS, Dijkstra, Bellman–Ford, MST algorithms, and flow algorithms). The emphasis is on algorithmic intuition, runtime analysis, and implementable variants—ideal for students seeking solid implementation and analysis skills.

33.2 How These Books Fit Together

These books have been crafted with a vision of progression and integration:

- **Logic:** Lays the theoretical foundation for computational reasoning.
- **Programming Basics:** Provides essential tools and concepts for coding.
- **Advanced Programming Skills:** Builds practical expertise for modern software challenges.
- **Algorithms and Data Structures:** Equips you with tools for writing efficient programs.
- **Computability and Complexity:** Teaches you to understand the limits and efficiencies of computation.

Together, they form a comprehensive learning pathway, from understanding the "why" to mastering the "how."

Stay in Touch

I hope you've enjoyed this journey and that it sparks a lifelong passion for programming and problem-solving. For updates on future books and projects, or to share your feedback, don't hesitate to connect.

Thank you once again, and happy coding!

Bibliography

[1] Joshua Bloch, *Effective Java*, 3rd edition, Addison-Wesley, Boston, 2018.

[2] Bruce Eckel, *Thinking in Java*, 4th edition, Prentice Hall, 2006.

[3] James Gosling, Bill Joy, Guy Steele, Gilad Bracha, *The Java Language Specification*, Addison-Wesley, 2014.

[4] Erich Gamma, Richard Helm, Ralph Johnson, John Vlissides, *Design Patterns: Elements of Reusable Object-Oriented Software*, Addison-Wesley, 1994.

[5] Ken Arnold, James Gosling, David Holmes, *The Java Programming Language*, 4th edition, Addison-Wesley, 2005.

[6] Paul Deitel, Harvey Deitel, *Java: How to Program*, 11th edition, Pearson, 2017.

[7] Kathy Sierra, Bert Bates, *Head First Java*, 2nd edition, O'Reilly, 2005.

[8] Robert C. Martin, *Clean Code: A Handbook of Agile Software Craftsmanship*, Prentice Hall, 2008.

Chapter 34

Imprint

Bibliographic information from the German National Library:
The German National Library lists this publication in the German National Bibliography; detailed bibliographic data can be accessed online at `https://dnb.de`.

Publishing:
BoD · Books on Demand GmbH,
Überseering 33,
22297 Hamburg,
bod@bod.de

Printing:
Libri Plureos GmbH,
Friedensallee 273,
22763 Hamburg

ISBN: 978-3-6963-8001-4